AN OLD HUNTSMAN'S
GUIDE TO DEER PURSUIT

An Old Huntsman's Guide to Deer Pursuit: Learn from Someone Else's Successes, Mistakes and Observations

Copyright © 2020 J. Wm. Peyton

ISBN: 9798696666457

A Publication of Tall Pine Books

|| *tallpinebooks.com*

*Published in the United States of America

AN OLD HUNTSMAN'S GUIDE TO DEER PURSUIT

LEARN FROM SOMEONE ELSE'S SUCCESSES,
MISTAKES AND OBSERVATIONS

J. WM. PEYTON

TALL PINE

This book is dedicated to:

My maternal grandfather, William, and my older brother, Jim (Jimmie Lee), both gone now; who taught me to hunt and to love hunting;

And

My departed friends and former hunting partners Dick and Ed, who shared my love of the outdoors, my passion for hunting and their families' traditional hunting grounds.

CONTENTS

1. Life as a Country Boy Hunter   1
2. Why Do I Hunt?   15
3. Sometimes They Are Incredibly Stupid!   19
4. Pay Attention to What a Doe Tells You!   25
5. Be Prepared   31
6. Do Not Assume   37
7. Know What is Legal   41
8. Reload   45
9. Sometimes Your Gear Fails You   51
10. B.R.A.S.S.   59
11. The Tree Stand   71
12. Don't Be Impulsive   83
13. The Bet   87
14. Be Courteous   93
15. Irony on Opening Day   99
16. The Unanticipated   107
17. What Have I Learned?   115
18. Trophy Hunting   135
19. After Action Reports   141
20. You Are So Very Special!   145
21. From Eden to Nod   151
22. Around the Corner   155
23. Moments in Life   157

About the Author   161

LIFE AS A COUNTRY BOY HUNTER

I grew up in a house that my father built; adding rooms as he and mom added family members and as money allowed. A large chicken coop was the only structure on the property when my parents bought it shortly after World War II. Dad converted that hut into a two room house with a well and an outhouse in the backyard. He, mom and my older brother, Jimmie, occupied it. The first addition, a kitchen and bedroom, happened when I came along two years later. I was nursed on milk still warm from a neighbor's cow; and later ate from the garden in the back yard; with the rest of the family. I grew into a sturdy kid; so when I turned eight, dad made me his "house-building apprentice" along with Jimmie. By then, dad had added another bedroom and a bath.

The house was sited five miles north of town; on a one acre plot of ground in a part of the county known as "Gobblers Knob." It was one mile from the local grade school. Five of my siblings and I walked to and from school regardless of weather. My parents only had one car, which dad took to work daily. Mom did not learn how to drive until I was 13 or 14 years old. She was a "stay at home mom;" like every other mom we knew except our school teachers.

Mom made all of our bread and pastries from scratch. She washed our dirty clothes in the basement, using a wringer machine with two rinse tubs. Then carried the baskets of wet laundry to the back yard and hung it on several clothes lines strung there. I caught my chin on one of those lines while playing chase one evening; and quickly found myself lying on my back with the wind knocked out of me. In the snowiest parts of winter, she hung the clothes from lines strung in the basement.

Mom sewed and "took in ironing" as side jobs for a little extra money through the year. She also mated our tame rabbits in time to sell baby bunnies to city folk around Easter each year. Those sales helped pay for our Easter clothes.

We kept mom busy ALL of the time. Mom treated the chiggers we kids got while picking black berries in a nearby field with alcohol and fingernail polish. I can still close my eyes and feel that fire! ...the chigger itches too, for that matter. I do not remember how she got the stains out of our skin after the black walnut harvest in the fall. We suffered the minor ailments: cuts and bruises, poison ivy, bee and wasp stings and colds; and my broken arm from falling out of a tree. We also weathered the serious diseases: German measles, chicken pox, mumps and tonsillitis (my first surgery). My youngest brother caught spinal meningitis when he was about six months old - and we nearly lost him. We did lose Ann Marie, at three days old. She was born prematurely. Her loss hit mom really hard - dad too, I guess, though he never spoke about it.

Our property was bounded on three sides by pasture fence, but was open to the road. Our front yard was bordered by a gravel and oil covered, county road. Two cars could pass, but each driver had to hug the road's edge. A drainage ditch about six feet wide and three feet deep abutted each side of the road. A car would occasionally wind up in that ditch; especially in winter.

Annually, just before school let out for summer, a county maintenance crew used a road grader to clean the ditches of weeds and debris. They added a new layer of crushed rock to the road and sprayed heavy, black oil on its surface. I invariably got a spanking for getting that "tar" on my bare feet. I sincerely believe that I learned to dance, at least in part, at the end of a cherry switch.

The road crew's activities were exciting for me to watch; but not nearly as exciting as watching operators use a variety of types of heavy equipment to build Interstate 55. The road bed was constructed about a half mile from my house during 1962. I was particularly interested during the summer and fall of 1963, while I watched them build the interstate bridges over the historic Sangamon River, which Abe Lincoln had navigated a little over a century earlier. When the crews finished those, they moved on north toward Chicago and I moved on to other interests. That was the only highway over which I ever drove more than 100 miles per hour - but that is yet another story.

Our one-half acre garden, behind the house, provided most of the vegetables that we ate through the year. We grew totally organic; with no herbicides, insecticides or chemical fertilizers. My parents could not afford to buy any of that stuff. We used "natural" fertilizers; the dung produced by our chickens and rabbits, and manure collected from a farm nearby. It was an aromatic, but very effective mix. I am wryly reminded of that today when I see the prices for "organic" food items in my local grocery stores.

At some point in time, dad built a shack next to the garden and divided it into a chicken coop and rabbit shed with entrances at each end. There, mom raised rabbits and chickens for food and barter. Neither I nor my siblings were allowed to have a pet chicken or rabbit; because one does not name one's food.

My parents bought three or four dozen chicks around Easter of every year. They were allowed run of the back yard all spring; and the back yard and garden in summer and early fall, when the plants grew sufficiently large. The chickens fed on the insects that plagued the vegetables, helped aerate the ground in the garden by constantly scratching the earth and left droppings that added nutrients to the soil. Between the yard and garden, they easily found enough bugs, weeds, grasses, and seeds to stay healthy.

Dad had to fence off the tomato plants with chicken wire to protect them; but the fowl posed no other problems - except to bare footed kids, which we all were all summer until school started. We kids, literally, only wore shoes on Sunday mornings; which saved dad and mom money that would otherwise have been spent on new pairs. I wore dad's second pair of shoes issued annually by the factory where he worked from about age eight to 13; when my feet got too big.

Mom canned vegetables for a couple weeks every fall;

with dad's active help. Her mom made jellies and preserves. When the canning was completed, "dress out" day happened for the chickens and rabbits.

Every fall, after "dress out" day, mom would barter canned vegetables, jellies, preserves, "dressed" chickens and "dressed" rabbits with the farmer that lived about a mile from us for freshly butchered beef. Our pork came from her father's sty.

In addition to jellies and preserves, grandma made the cottage cheese and butter that we used daily. Occasionally, I had to help churn butter; and have no nostalgic memories of that drudgery. Grandma also hand stitched beautiful quilts from odd pieces of cloth. My seven siblings and I each got the one she had made for us, individually, when she passed away.

We had a family tradition of visiting New Salem, Illinois, every summer. That was the village where Abraham Lincoln lived from 1831 to 1837, before moving to Springfield. Grandma (mom's mom) always drew a crowd of spectators as she walked us through the village and quietly explained every item on display. She had used each in her youth and, in fact, used many around her home into the early 1960's.

Mom's parents were natives of south-central Kentucky, who migrated north to central Illinois in the early 1920's so grandpa could work the coal mines. He was a non-union miner; my dad's dad was a union miner. He considered mom's dad "scab" because he worked the mines when the unions were striking. In their prime, my grandfathers had no use for each other. Like most men at that time, both carried pocket pistols; but survived each other. Somehow mom and dad still got together. I see that as a happy version of "Romeo and Juliet." Both grandpas mellowed in later life and tolerated each other well.

Our family often visited our Kentucky relatives. We commonly went in spring to assist with the tobacco and corn planting; sometimes in late summer to early fall for the harvests. Occasionally, we went both times. Corn planting was not too hard. We just walked behind the plow and dropped a seed about every foot along the row. The hard part was carrying a fairly heavy bag seeds slung over the shoulder for hours at a time. Riding the tobacco seedling planter meant muddy, wrinkled hands, broken finger nails, bruised fingers and skinned knuckles.

If we went in the heat of August, we helped with the tobacco crop. Cutting the tobacco stalks was hot, hazardous, back breaking work. Then we had to pierce the base of the stalks and slide them, one after another onto long sticks. At least that was done in the shade of the barn. The very risky part of the process was hanging those heavy sticks in the tiers of a tobacco barn. The men did that because you had to be both strong and sure footed to work 20 feet off the barn floor.

If we went in late September or early October, we helped harvest the corn. We shucked corn by hand, using a hook that was attached to a leather half-glove. As I remember it, the process went thusly: reach in the top of the husk and grab the ear with your left hand; cut the base of the husk with the hook using your right hand; pull the ear out of the husk; throw it over your left shoulder into a wagon that is pulled along the corn row at a slow walk speed by a mule team or tractor. Try that for a day if you want to really experience shoulder and arm pain.

After the harvest came the chopping and stacking of

the stalks. Using wide bladed corn knives was dangerous, especially when you got tired. They later got collected and ground for fodder.

We also helped in making sorghum. I clearly remember paddling sorghum (stirring it with a boat paddle) in a hot vat. It sat over an open fire near the shed that housed the crushing machine that was belt-powered by a flywheel tractor. I had to help stir for hours to keep the sorghum from sticking and burning until it was cooked down. We took many quart jars of the syrup home for our efforts. Oh my, how good it tasted! Most of the sorghum plants were allowed to mature and the grain heads were harvested and ground into flour. The cattle and pigs got the stalks.

Dad's ancestors were living in the Springfield, Illinois, area when Abraham Lincoln moved there from New Salem. The men on both sides of dad's family fought for the Union in the Civil War and proudly voted for "Honest Abe." My father's great-grandfather, Cuthbert Peyton, lost his life in that war. His great-grandfather, George James, lost his left leg. George became a shoe cobbler and also carved prosthetic legs he sold to war veterans for extra income. Dad always said that grandpa James adamantly insisted his entire adult life that their branch of the family was not related to those "Missouri Jameses" (Jesse and Frank).

As soon as school recessed for summer, when I was 16 years old, my parents moved back to the neighborhood in town in which they had grown up. Dad could look across the alley from the "new" house and see the house in which he had been born. The "old" house we left was a ranch style house with a large, eat-in kitchen, a living room, four bedrooms, one full and two half baths, a nearly full, unfinished basement and a screened in porch that spanned 20 feet across the front. A two bay garage sat next to the house; connected by a short, open breezeway. One bay was walled off from the other; and built out as an electronics workshop where dad repaired televisions, radios and small appliances after his regular day job.

The "new" house was a two story structure that was almost 100 years old. It had four small rooms and a bath downstairs and two small bedrooms, a bathroom and a glassed in porch upstairs. It also had a partial basement that was unfinished. Dad's great grandfather, George, had owned it. The shed where he made and sold shoes and legs sat next to the alley in the small back yard. Remodeling of that "new" house began immediately after we moved in and continued for about ten years.

When I was 21, my paternal grandfather asked me to witch a well for him. It was then that I learned that when I was three years old, it was somehow determined that I could witch water. The four wells that I witched were the only ones in the neighborhood (about a dozen houses in a mile length of county road) that did not go dry every summer.

My father and his father never hunted. Dad could never bring himself to even kill a chicken or rabbit during fall "dress out" day - mom took care of that; with my active assistance from about age eight on. Which reminds me of the most memorable spanking I got from mom when I was a kid (corporal punishment was the order of the day when I grew up).

I remember not so much because of the severity of it (she swatted me several times with her hand); rather, because I felt offended to have received it. She gave it to me for "being disrespectful." But I was the proxy recipient for dad.

It was "dress out" day for the chickens and rabbits. Mom was both fast and agile. She could catch the chickens; and would wring their necks. Their heads would detach during that process. When this happened, the chickens' bodies would have seizures. Their legs and wings would vigorously twitch and jerk for up to two minutes before they settled.

When they settled, dad would gather them and douse each in hot water (hot to the touch, never boiling) that he kept in a caldron borrowed for the purpose from mom's parents. It sat on a grate over a fire in the back yard. My job was to run around and herd the chickens toward mom.

When all of the chickens were dispatched, all three of us would pluck them; and mom and I would gut them. Dad would then rinse them in clean, ice water and lay them out on a table to air dry before wrapping them in butcher paper ahead of placing in the freezer. After the chickens, we conducted a similar process for the rabbits. Mom and I killed, skinned and gutted them, and dad rinsed and wrapped them; then they also went to the freezer. We stretched and cured the rabbit hides over racks dad made from coat hangers; then dad sold them somewhere.

On this particular day, one headless chicken's convulsions caused it to bound under the hem of mom's dress. Mom only wore dresses; dresses that reached to mid-calf; and saddle shoes with white cotton socks. Off she went, yelling and shrieking, across the yard, desperately trying to escape; with that chicken hopping and flapping between her legs. Dad fell on the ground laughing; so I started laughing too. To say the least, mom failed to find the humor in her circumstance!

So I got spanked for being disrespectful while dad lamely tried to talk her out of punishing me. He was careful to stay out of her reach, though - mom could throw a mean right jab. That is another, unrelated story... and, no, she never used it on dad (to my knowledge) or us kids. Girls who grew up during the Great Depression were tough!

Life as a hunter started early for this country boy, growing up in central Illinois in the 1950's. When I was five, I got a BB gun for Christmas. Not a "Red Rider," but my greatest treasure for years. My maternal grandfather and my older brother taught me how to shoot it.

I can still clearly remember the adrenaline rush that I got the first time that I aimed that BB gun at a bird; a male sparrow with a black patch of feathers on his chest. I remember that because I also remember the engulfing feeling of shame I felt when I watched him fall after I shot. In that moment, I lost an innocence that I had not realized I had... I had crossed a threshold, never able to return.

By age six, I was routinely killing the sparrows and starlings that caused such a fire hazard by roosting in the eaves of houses in my rural neighborhood; and I was playing beagle for my older brother. I struggled through the briars and brush piles to scare the rabbits out under my brother's deadly fire. I also circled hickory and oak trees so squirrels would move around away from me to where he quietly waited to take them home for supper. We often provided the meat (squirrel and rabbit; an occasional young groundhog) for supper during the fall and early winter that brought variety to our diet. The morels in spring and puff ball mushrooms in fall were treats Jimmie and I also hunted in the woods. We ate turkey on Thanksgiving and Christmas; ham was for Easter.

Eight was a magical age because it was then that I got his Montgomery Ward, single shot, 16 Gauge shotgun; and the right to hunt rather than be the "beagle." Fifteen years passed before I bought my first pump shotgun, a Ted Williams Model 200 12 Gauge from Sears Roebuck and Company.

It became my constant hunting companion until late 1987, when I took up the challenge of hunting with a 20 Gauge shot gun. It is a Mossberg 500 Country Squire that I bought, used, from a hunting buddy. I still rely on it during all "gun" hunting seasons.

I am a devoted short-range weapon user who believes that marksmanship and woodcraft skill are equally important. I developed a terminal case of deer hunting fever in the mid 1970's. I have taken over 60 deer with gun and bow. I do not own any trophy mounts. I do not intentionally hunt alpha bucks; though I fully understand the challenge that they offer. I have the highest regard for the hunter who has the skill and determination to succeed at such a hunt. I simply have never found a recipe where I can cook antlers and make them tender enough to eat; so I do not care about the buck's rack.

I am a meat hunter. I caught the hunting bug from my maternal grandfather; who hunted squirrel, rabbit, raccoon, ground hog and even the rare opossum - but strictly for food. He taught me never to kill an animal unless I ate it. My quarry is the one to three year old buck or doe deer. It is easier to hunt, usually easier to drag, and has more tender, succulent loins. I do not go to any great length to take advantage of my prey; but I do have a lot of respect for its senses and natural survival skills. I am also a firm believer that a sportsman will properly prepare him - or her - self before hunting season for the expected encounter; and strive to make a quick, clean kill.

My son did not care to hunt from age five to nearly forty; so many years that I gave up the hope that we would ever share time in the field. That was his choice. I felt obligated to respect and never comment upon it. I believe that I know why he did not hunt. He does not like to be cold, even today. And the first time I shot a rabbit, while he attended me on the hunt, he was both startled and frightened by the utterly unexpected noise. He had his head down, trudging through what for his five year old legs was deep snow when the rabbit jumped and I shot. The noise of that 12 gauge was so loud and surprising that he stumbled and fell; face down, into the snow. Cold, alarmed and humiliated, his first hunt was a total disaster from his perspective.

I do not know why he changed his mind and hunts so avidly now; but I delight in every chance we have to be together in the field or a hunting blind fashioning shared memories.

Sixty plus years after I killed my first sparrow, I watched as the older of my two grandsons nearly retched while he wrestled with that guilty feeling after he killed his first squirrel. We talked about that while sitting at the base of the tree from which that squirrel had fallen. Our shared experiences added one more tie that binds us together across the span of generations. He is now 13, and as avid a deer hunter as his father and I.

The younger of my grandsons told me when he was six, "Grandpa, deer hunting is great - until you have to gut the deer." He has been doggedly accompanying us on hunts since he was four; and has helped clean squirrel and rabbit and field dress deer. He seems to love hunting already; but I believe his penchant for spinning a yarn will ultimately make him more a fisherman than hunter. He recently turned eight; the magic age when his dad will allow him to hunt his first deer... more shared memories of life impacting experiences soon to be filed in the heart. None of my three granddaughters are the least interested in hunting or shooting sports, at least for now.

Hunting teaches very serious and, I believe essential, life lessons. I am not a professional hunter; but have walked my share of trails in 67 plus years in the field. I am not much of an Aesop either, but I have written some short stories that I now offer to you to emphasize some deer hunting tips that I have learned through successes; and, more often, mistakes in the field.

2

WHY DO I HUNT?

I have loved being in the woods and watching wildlife going about their lives since I was about five years old. I want to pass the opportunity to enjoy those experiences along to my grandchildren and great-grandchildren.

I also care about the health and welfare of the animals that I observe. I know that the best way to preserve an animal species is to put it on the menu. This sounds crazy, I admit, but look at the animals with the greatest populations and maximum support from humans - the farm animals - cattle, swine, sheep, goats, chickens, ducks and geese. If people value a particular animal as food, or a source of income, they work toward, and invest in, that animal's welfare.

Throughout Africa today, human populations are rapidly rising. All forms of wildlife are facing severe challenges due to loss of habitat and predation by locals trying to protect their families, homes and crops. Many African governments have struggled to find a way to preserve wildlife while balancing the needs - and wants - of ever increasing numbers of citizens. The only long term successes these governments have met are by introducing regulated game hunting. This has the dual benefit of bringing revenue to the government through licenses and fees AND; more importantly, causing the local peoples to value the wildlife around them as a major source of their income.

In ancient times, shepherds performed tremendous service to their communities. They faced a wide assortment of hazards while caring for the animals that were so essential to the townsfolk for food, clothing and even religious purposes. But shepherds became known as liars and tellers of tall tales because they had experiences and encounters, while tending the flocks and herds, which those city dwellers could hardly envisage and never understood. The urbanites shunned the very people who were supporting the literal sustenance of their lives and livelihoods. City dwellers saw shepherds as unsophisticated, scruffy and untrustworthy. The truth was that shepherds had far richer lives because they occupied two worlds, simultaneously. They had a sweeping range of experiences beyond the imaginations of the parochial townsmen.

North American hunters perform services very similar to shepherds of ancient times. Our ancestors eliminated most of the large North American predators; the bear, lion, and wolf in particular, because those large carnivores preyed on humans. People wanted to make the places where they lived safe for their families. Throughout the vast majority of deer range here in North America, we hunters are the only predators left to keep the size of deer herds in check. We prevent deer deaths on massive scales from starvation and disease. Healthy deer need hunters to cull the herd and maintain an appropriate population balance that the local habitat will support.

The hundreds of species of other, non-game animals, birds and insects that live in deer habitat benefit directly from the efforts made by and funded by hunters. Plants benefit from hunters' contributions to habitat development. Whole watersheds benefit.

The soil and water quality of impacted areas are improved. The risks of and from forest fires are substantially mitigated through management efforts funded by hunters and hunting related activities.

In less than ten minutes research on the internet, I gathered the following statistical information about the economic contributions of hunters and hunting. Hunting funds conservation AND the economy. Communities across our nation and ALL forms of wildlife and plant life benefit dramatically from sportsmen and women every year. It generates more than 38 BILLION dollars a year in retail spending for hunting equipment and accessories, hunter travel, food and lodging costs and a host of other hunting related fees and expenses. Further, hunters pay the most to support wildlife habitat. They fund wildlife on a vastly larger scale than any other group. Habitat, research and wildlife law enforcement work are all paid for by hunters. This materially helps both hunted and non-game species.

Additionally, through state licenses and fees, hunters pay nearly $800,000,000 a year for conservation programs; and donate almost $450,000,000 a year to conservation efforts. When the $370,000,000 plus in taxes on guns, ammunition, bows and arrows - *that* **hunters** *actually* **requested** *to be levied* - is added; the total amount of money contributed to wildlife programs of all types by hunters, exclusively, is over **$1,600,000,000 every *year*!**

Whitetail deer are far and away the American farmers' worst problem. Farmers suffer tens (possible hundreds) of billions of dollars in losses each year due to crop damage caused by deer. They desperately need hunters to reduce these massive losses - that, by the way, drive food prices up.

Private automobile and truck drivers, commercial truck drivers and transportation companies benefit from deer hunting activity. Untold numbers of people are involved in crashes because of deer every year. It is estimated that more than one million deer-vehicle collisions occur annually in the United States. These collisions lead to over 200 human deaths, about 29,000 serious human injuries and $1.1 billion in property damage every year. State and federal governments, insurance companies, and drivers spend an additional $3 billion in an effort to reduce and manage the increasing number of deer-vehicle collisions. Do not forget the huge number of law enforcement and emergency services personnel who must respond to these crashes rather than protect us in other ways.

If you do not hunt, then join us. Please come out and go hunting - give the sport a try. If you are a hunter, keep hunting and reach out to others; invite non-hunters to join in on a hunting experience. Hunting provides different life experiences and opportunities that will expand your life view and offer chances to appreciate new horizons - and incredible vistas.

This is part of why I hunt. The other reasons will reveal themselves as you read...

3

SOMETIMES THEY ARE INCREDIBLY STUPID!

It was opening day of deer season. I was in my ladder stand on Hoosier National Forest land in southern Indiana before first light. The water had frozen in my canteen by 9am. The wind had been strong from the northwest since midnight, but the predicted snow had not come. By 11:30 that morning, I was in bad need of some coffee and other forms of relief. I climbed down from my ladder stand and headed to camp a half mile away. I was moving slowly through open hardwoods, about half way there, when the wind suddenly dropped and big, fluffy flakes began to fall. By the time I cleared the trees the ground had turned white. Snowfalls on opening day of gun season are rare events where I hunt. My partners and I had talked about the chance of snow and what it might mean for the hunt the night before. I had read that deer do crazy things during a gentle snow and was anxious to find out if that was true. Besides, I had taken a lot of ribbing when I shared the feeling that I would fill both of my tags on opening day; and I was eager to prove that I could.

I hurried into the camper and gulped a large cup of hot coffee, which helped get a sandwich down faster. My hunting partners were lounging in the warmth, and watching me with puzzled looks. When I headed for the door, one asked, "Where're you going'" "On stand." was my hurried reply as I started through the door. "You're crazy going' out in this." he said, pointing with a thumb through the window behind where he was sitting to the heavily falling snow. "Can't kill deer in a trailer." was my response. What he said to that isn't repeatable.

I jog-walked back up the logging trail, which was the fastest way to reach my stand; I cut into the woods a few minutes later, and slowed to a walk for the last 200 yards to my destination. I avoid walking on deer trails because I don't like to leave my scent on their main highways. This time I was in a hurry and had seen no fresh tracks on this particular trail the three times I had examined it in the past week, including the previous afternoon. Besides, it offered the quietest approach route to my stand. I took the trail and the chance.

Reaching my stand, I tied off my shotgun and carefully climbed the ten metal rungs, which by now were slick with snow. I got settled, and hoisted my 20-gauge, pump shotgun. After loading, I cradled it across my left arm and opened my coat to vent the excess heat I had built up in my rush. I carefully scanned the two trails to my left that had shown fresh tracks yesterday. The wind was calm, coming across the trails to me, and the snow was falling at a steady rate, almost vertically from a gray sky. I caught a movement out the corner of my right eye.

It did not make sense. The doe was walking through the small clearing which I had crossed not 10 minutes before, on the very trail that I had used to my stand. Average size, slightly taller than a big German shepherd, she was long legged and graceful in her brown-gray winter coat and had a surprising amount of white hair on her throat and chest. She gently blew steam from nostrils into the cold air with each breath. My appreciation quickly turned to mild apprehension when I realized that she was on my wrong side.

My gun was lying across my lap, muzzle to the left, pointing toward those promising trails. Very slowly, I rose out of my slouch, and started to shift the gun to my left shoulder for the shot.

I had nearly finished when she sensed my movement and locked her eyes on me. I froze. She crouched slightly and stared intently at me for several seconds. I held my breath and waited, mind racing, trying to think of how I could get my bead on her when she bolted. I had played the movements through several times when she relaxed, twitched her tail, glanced back over her shoulder, and started walking. I could not believe my luck! I would get a shot, though it would not be an easy one. She changed direction and started strolling to my left; towards the heavy growth of pines that bordered the hardwoods I had chosen to stand hunt. The shotgun was in my left shoulder and I knew that I would not have the chance to switch back to my natural right-hand hold before she disappeared. She turned to her left and started walking into those open hardwoods! I shifted my body, aimed in, safety off now, wait for a good opening through the trees. She turned again! Now she was walking directly away from me. I hate to take this type of shot, but I was looking down on her and had a good view of her back and shoulder areas. I kept the bead on her back, just behind her shoulders, as I started to squeeze. She was about 40 yards out, and starting down a moderate slope. I fired. She threw her flag in the air and hurled herself through the trees directly away from me. I chambered another shell, aimed hurriedly, and fired again. She was gone.

Cursing myself under my breath for not dropping her with either shot, I started to bring the gun back to my lap to reload when I caught another movement out of that right eye. Hardly daring to move at all, I turned my head as slowly as my patience would allow, while straining to shift my eyes right as far as possible. There he stood! Right in the middle of the small clearing that the doe had left only a minute or two before, staring holes through me. Tense as a bow string, but not as much as I, he stood for what seemed an eternity, shifting his head from side to side in an obvious effort to make visual sense out of the large, still object 20 yards away and 12 feet up, that had just made so much noise.

"Why hadn't I realized he was probably back there?" ran through my mind repeatedly as I waited to see what he would do next - though I already thought I knew. Still, with all of the noise and movement that I had made, I should never have seen him in the first place; maybe I would get a shot after all. Finally, he too seemed to relax. He shifted his stare into the direction that the doe had fled. I took a big chance and moved ever so slightly. In a blur, he reversed direction and charged back down the trail that I had used what seemed at once like seconds and hours ago. "He never raised his flag." was my mental comment as I sat and watched helplessly. A minute later, I heard four shots ring out from the area to which he had run.

I am one hunter who always assumes that he hit the animal at which he shot. I unloaded my shotgun and lowered it to the ground before carefully joining it. After reloading and rechecking the safety, I headed for the spot where I had seen the doe when I fired the first time.

I checked the ground and surrounding foliage carefully for over 100 yards of her clearly visible snow tracks. Nothing. Thoroughly frustrated with myself, I returned to my perch and nursed my wounded pride. I had nearly convinced myself that I had totally ruined my only chance for a deer on this stand and this day, when I noticed a doe heading in my direction on the very tracks that I had made while searching.

She was some distance out, but definitely headed my way, and at a good pace. She was less than 15 yards away when a single slug from my gun put an almost instant end to her journey. I had watched her for some time because I could not quite believe what I was seeing. Not only should she not have been walking along my trail; she had a crease along her back, starting at the center at the rear of her rib cage and angling slightly until it ended over her right shoulder. This was the doe that I had missed! My slug had shaved the hair off her back, leaving what appeared to be a perfect part.

I started to climb down from my stand when it occurred to me that if she had been stupid enough to return with her hair parted, that buck just might have survived the shots I had heard and could come looking for her. I waited for 15 minutes before I saw him coming towards us from my right rear, at an impossible angle for a shot. I shifted to my left, raised the gun to my right shoulder, twisted as far in his direction as I could, and waited. He didn't make me wait long. I took him with a single shot, at about 15 yards from me, and 20 yards from the doe. I climbed down, tagged both deer, and tackled an immensely rewarding field dressing job.

I am convinced that if I had not carted both deer to camp by 1:00pm, as I did, my hunting partners would never have believed my story either.

4

PAY ATTENTION TO WHAT A DOE
TELLS YOU!

The first year that I hunted with a bow, I was sitting on the back of a very large mound of dirt that covered an ammunition storage bunker on a military reservation in southern Indiana. This being my initial hunt in the area, I had chosen the spot because it provided the optimum vantage point from which to examine my assigned hunting area. Seated just below the crest of this hill amid a growth of briars, I had excellent concealment and a premium view. About 12 yards below me was a trail that, from its size, I took to be used by the cattle that grazed in the meadows that virtually surrounded me. Slightly further to my front was a steep, but shallow ravine through which flowed a small stream. Beyond this was a growth of mature oak trees that marched up the opposite knoll and blotted out the skyline.

Just after eight in the morning, a large group of does left the tree line 200 yards to my left front and sauntered boldly in a column across the meadow in my general direction. The lead deer was noticeably larger than the others, and drew my attention almost immediately. Hoping for the possibility of a shot, I studied the ground to their front and only then noticed the trail that meandered to a junction with the path below my location. Filled with anticipation, I watched impatiently as they came on. The group was drawing fairly near when I realized that the first doe had looked over her left shoulder several times to the tree line she had recently left. Curious, I started glancing back there also, while giving her most of my notice. That is why I nearly did not see the large buck that was moving along a parallel trail in the trees to my front.

With a wide and thick 14-point rack, he was a serious deer! After the initial jolt of adrenaline cleared my system, I now started to worry that the does would turn in my direction onto the trail below me; as I was fervently hoping they would just seconds earlier. Focused now on my monarch, I threw nervous glances toward them until they turned away onto a previously unnoticed trail. It ran along a draw that crossed the path and led to the road on which I had parked in front of the bunker. I worried that the sight of the car would spook them for far longer than I probably needed to be. No alarm came. He made tediously slow progress. I had ample time to find the faint trail he was using, and note that it too joined the path below me. Quickly choosing the spot where I wanted him to be when I took my shot, my mind fixed on my inexperience at bow hunting, and how little preparation I had actually accomplished. My worry was justified, but served only to goad me to serious practice later.

A young buck came over the bunker, feeding on the berries, and practically walked up my back. He made so much noise that he frightened the mature buck that quickly bounded into denser cover. I watched my chance for sweet success melt away with him like chocolate in the hot, midday sun. I too thought that another hunter had blundered into my area. That is until I glared over my right shoulder into the young buck's chest, rather than the human face I was expecting.

He turned and leapt from sight before I could regain my composure.

Two seasons later, I was slumped on my seat with a cold drizzle beating monotonously over my rubber parka. It was nearly 10:30 am, and only the memory of a predicted break in the weather kept my hopes for seeing anything move alive.

Stubbornly hunkered in, I was not prepared for the doe's sudden appearance on a trail perpendicular to the one I had been watching. She was about 35 yards away before she either saw or, more likely, smelled me. Her snort brought me out of my stupor with a start. I only had time to think about how large her tail was before she disappeared.

Thoroughly disgusted at myself for being detected so easily, I took her clear hint that I was in a poor location, and decided to relocate my stand in a better site a few yards away. I rose and moved another 10 or 15 yards from my chosen trail into thicker cover. The rain had been tapering off for some time, so I decided to strip off my noisy rain gear and trade the risk of getting soaked for the advantages of freer, quieter movement.

I will never figure out why he came shuffling along with his nose to the ground, grunting. No other doe had moved on any trail within sight since before sunrise. Even if one had, the rain would have washed the scent away hours before. He was not even on my chosen trail, but was moving parallel to it about 20 yards closer to me than I had expected. I had no more than sat down when I saw him. It was not possible for him not to have heard neither her loud snort nor the noise I had made removing my rain gear. Besides, I had just been moving around! What I could see of his rack was promising, so I took the shot. He fell a scant 12 paces from where I sat. When I walked up to him, I realized that what appeared to be a very respectable ten pointer had five large tines on the right side of his rack, and a spike on the left.

Seven or eight years later, I was again sitting in the cold rain, wryly recalling the weatherman's promise of clearing around midmorning. This was a persistent downpour that limited my vision to about 50 yards through open hardwoods that normally offered an easy view for well over three times that distance. Only the determination to outlast my hunting partners had kept me on stand as late as I was.

At first, I did not see the doe come out of the heavy cover about 30 yards to my right and start down the long slope of the hillside that I was watching. Her gray coat melded with her surroundings so well in the poor light that the rain nearly shielded her from view. She jogged about 15 yards before she stopped and looked back, nearly turning completely around in the process. Proceeding into the open hardwoods, her quickened gait carried her promptly down the hill, angling slightly toward me. Since one member of my hunting party had taken a stand in the general direction from which she had come, I assumed that he had spooked her to me. I did not check the area that she had left for more than a few seconds, looking for an orange vest, before fixing my attention and sights on her.

Several things happened at almost the same time when I fired. She tumbled, then instantly rose in a headlong rush. I ejected the spent cartridge and chambered another while trying to track her with the bead of my shotgun sight. I caught a blur of movement in the corner of my right eye and shifted my focus to try to determine what was moving out there behind her. The huge buck, now only about 20 yards away, whirled and fled back to the thick cover. I mentally cursed myself for not paying greater heed to the clear signal that someone or something was behind her. I shifted my attention back to the doe and ended her stumbling flight while my mind replayed the picture of his beautiful rack.

5

BE PREPARED

Squirrels are brazen little beasts who seem to be everywhere during deer season. For deer hunters, they are beautiful, mischievous, playful, inquisitive banes. Have you ever truly studied a squirrel at close range, when it did not know that you were there?

Did you notice how it uses it tail? I don't mean just as a rudder to help it make sharp turns at a full run or a counterbalance to steady itself as it moves through the trees. I am talking about when it uses its tail for a parasol to shade itself in the bright sun, a stole to cover itself in a cold wind, or a warning flag to others of its kind when they venture into the wrong territory.

Did you realize that by watching its tail, you could almost read the squirrel's mind? If it is squatting on a limb with its tail twitching rhythmically in large flowing, vertical "S" shaped motions, staring across a gap to another branch; you can almost hear it saying, "Can I make this jump?" When a squirrel is up on all four legs with its tail rapidly cycling up and down, but never rising above the horizontal plane, you know that it is irritated. Jerky, side-to-side movements tell you that the squirrel is both uneasy about a situation and uncertain about how to deal with it.

Have you watched it take a dust bath scant feet beneath you? Have you noticed how thoroughly it will inspect and investigate every nook of a tree? Or notice how starkly white its underside is? Have you marveled at the ease with which it can open a hickory nut or black walnut?

Did a squirrel ever casually walk across your boots? Or sit almost within touching distance and study you? Have you sat helplessly as it hid in a nearby tree and screamed its danger cry incessantly while you waited in vain for it to be quiet again?

Did you ever pivot your head so slowly that it seemed to take minutes to swivel it a quarter turn, while your eyes ached from being forced to look impossibly far to the side, thinking that you just heard a deer, only to discover old twitching tail burrowing around in the leaves for acorns. Then, relaxed, you swing your head back around to discover a buck boring a hole into you with his eyes because your unguarded movement caught his attention?

Maybe you were watching a youngster dawdle in almost the same spot an older squirrel had been only a few minutes before, and saw the youth suddenly rear onto its hind legs, stare off behind you for a few seconds, then flee. When you turned, smiling in expectation of the pleasure in watching the dominate squirrel open the chase, a deer was standing in a perfect pose at an impossible angle to take a shot - watching you.

Possibly, you became convinced, because you could clearly detect every step that a tiny gray squirrel was taking along the ground 15 yards away, that the leaves were so dry a deer could never get close without being heard; then looked down and found yourself completely unprepared for the deer, which you suddenly noticed right under your tree stand.

Did you ever have a season of bow hunting for deer that ended with a tally of three badly cut up squirrels and one small spike buck? Did you say that you have been deer hunting?

Those annoying little gray squirrels had hounded me all morning as I sat 35 yards off a promising trail a quarter mile deep in a North Carolina swamp. The heat, wind, and mosquitoes combined to destroy my morale by 11:00am. I went back to camp, ate, and sat complaining to my hunting partner about those squirrels. He had suffered from them too, so we decided to spend the midday taking our frustrations out on them. A short time later, I was back on stand, this time looking for the squirrels. They had evaporated in the noon sun. For over two hours, I fought mosquitoes and watched in vain. Around 2:00pm, I got the feeling that I had better stay alert for deer. I opened the breech on my pump shot gun and removed the #6 shot shell, laying it on the ground beside a deer slug that I had removed from my pocket. Sitting flat on the ground under a huge pine, I only half expected to see anything, but kept up a visual sweep of the trees and the ground, just in case.

He came, nose to the trail, with the wind, at about 2:20pm. So small (just slightly over 100 pounds) that at first I thought he was a doe. His appearance did not trigger *any* action on my part for several tens of seconds. When he raised his head, I realized that I was watching a buck, "He's still in velvet." was driven from my thoughts by "HE! That's a buck!" I fumbled for the slug while he closed distance with an effortless gait. I shoved the shell home, and brought the gun to my shoulder, closing the breech in the same movement. When he heard the metallic clack, he turned toward me and froze. He was only 23 paces away when the slug hit him in the front of the chest. He collapsed back onto his rump and fell to his left side... a quick, clean kill.

On another occasion, I had sat at the base of a huge oak tree from about three in the afternoon until nearly dusk; plagued by squirrels searching the leaves all around me looking for acorns. By sundown, I had basically stopped reacting to the sound of rustling in the dry leaves. Having neither seen nor heard any deer in over four hours, I finally called the hunt and headed back to my truck.

Just as I entered the parking area, maybe 50 feet from the truck, I un-nocked the arrow from my bowstring. I was in the awkward process of putting the arrow into the quiver while walking, when I heard yet more rustling in the leaves to my right front. I took another step or two before I heard a snort and froze, almost in mid-stride. Bow in my left hand and arrow in my right, I moved my eyes as far right as I could and saw a four point buck staring at me from just in the tree line about 20 yards away. He could not have been more than 5 yards from my truck! There I stood, head turned left and down, right arm across my body, causing me to hunch slightly, feet at full stride separation and my eyes turned as far right as I could get them to go.

I believe that only the deer's young age and his resulting ignorance of man kept that buck from immediately bolting out of sight. The wind was in my favor, but the light and my position in the open were not.

I stood as statue still as I could, hardly daring to

breathe for what seemed minutes. Finally, he wagged his tail, then calmly turned and slowly walked in to the trees. Convinced that he was facing far enough away from me that he could not see my movements, I slowly shifted my position, nocked the arrow and drew my bow. By the time that I got the bow to full draw and aimed in his direction, I could no longer see him well enough to place the yardage pin for an accurate shot. I had the dubious pleasure of watching him stroll away through my bow sight. I had not been prepared for an encounter so close to my vehicle; and that had cost me a shot at a buck. Be mentally prepared to see deer any time you are outside your vehicle.

6

DO NOT ASSUME

I t had been a long, but beautiful morning on opening day of gun season. I had sat on my stool, hard against a large pine tree, since before first light. The wide, shallow valley which I had been watching had no less than four well used deer trails running parallel through it to the dense thicket about 80 yards to my right; that had been a clear-cut five years before. By 10:30am, the heat and wind had both risen noticeably. The wind had shifted, and was blowing diagonally from me to the thicket. I was getting hot and stiff, and was seriously thinking of returning to camp.

The single shot startled me. It came from directly across the valley; but I could neither see nor hear the hunter who had taken it. I soon did see a very large doe running directly at me, perpendicular to the trails. At her pace, she would run over me in a minute or two. I raised my gun and let her come on. About 50 yards out, she suddenly collapsed in a heap. I got the impression of another deer turning away from her to my right, but her unexpected fall had focused all of my attention on her; so I paid little heed. I assumed that it was a yearling doe and dismissed it from my mind.

I rose and walked a few feet to the low, natural, rock wall I had been looking over all morning. The doe lay in an odd position, partially buried by the leaves into which she had burrowed nose first when she fell. I decided to watch her and wait for the hunters, which I could now hear, to come.

That's why the next shot also startled me. Looking in the direction of this second shot, I clearly saw the buck. He was an average size four pointer. I had been so intent on the doe, that I had not noticed him. He was moving to my right toward the thick brush, but seemed to be in no particular hurry. He looked back toward the doe several times while I waited for the next shot I assumed would come.

After what seemed a long time, but was probably only 10 to 15 seconds, I decided that the next shot was not coming. I aimed and fired at the buck three separate times as he continued his run for cover. Each time he slowed, but did not fall. He tottered into the thick stand of brush and small trees as I hurriedly reloaded and excitedly walked after him.

I did not think that he would get very far, and I was right. Thirty or so feet in, I saw him struggle to rise. My fourth shot ended his flight. After field dressing, I discovered that all three of my first set of shots had struck the buck high in the chest cavity. They punctured the tops of both of his lungs.

This was my first year of hunting with a 20-gauge shotgun. Due to the distance at which I had fired (over 80 yards), I had expected the slugs to drop several inches before reaching him. They had maintained a much flatter trajectory, and I had nearly missed.

I later learned from the other hunters that the buck had been following the doe when she was shot. They had not seen him initially, and had assumed that the doe was alone. Surprised, they watched him follow her flight after the first shot until she fell; then veer off to their left, only to unexpectedly circle back toward her.

Both of these hunters were using muzzle-loading rifles. The first had shot the doe before he saw the buck, and had not had time to re-load. The second could not get a clear shot at the buck until it returned; which he had not expected, so he had rushed the shot and missed. Both had stood with empty weapons and watched the buck trot away. I had nearly done the same with a fully loaded pump shotgun!

Even though the other hunters had seen the buck first, neither objected to me having killed it. They had missed their chance at him and assumed the buck was lost to them anyway before they suddenly heard me shoot. We helped each other dress and drag the two deer out. We had a chance to discuss what had happened while on our way back to our respective camps. Our consensus was that the doe was in heat and the buck was tending her hard. He was so intently focused on her that he had paid no attention to us - until he was hit by my first slug; and it was too late. You might say that the buck "assumed" that he and the doe were alone...

7

KNOW WHAT IS LEGAL

I have hunted in a number of different states over the years. Each provided me with a set of regulations about the size of a small magazine at no cost. I have made it a point of personal pride to read these rules each time that I bought my license. I have never had any negative experiences with wardens, though I have been stopped many times; and been checked for proper licenses and tags, ammunition, the plug in my gun, and had my bag thoroughly examined for harvested game. I firmly believe that knowing the rules - and abiding by them - has always made my hunting experiences positive affairs. I do study the annual issue of regulations more thoroughly now than I did before.

A number of years ago, while still in the Marines, I was stationed at a large military base in North Carolina. When the time came to buy my hunting license, I learned that the state had a wonderful multiple species hunting license that allowed the hunter to buy all of the required licenses and permits in a single package. This included deer tags for all of the various seasons at one time. A comprehensive set of regulations came with the license. Since I hunted only with a bow and shotgun at the time, I did not pay much attention to the statutes pertaining to the other deer hunting seasons. This turned out to be a costly mistake.

My military duties included assigning people to temporary jobs away from their normal work routine. Several of those jobs were assisting the game warden, on a monthly basis, during the hunting seasons. I saw this as a great job, so I selected someone who had been working hard for me, and who enjoyed hunting. I assigned him to the first month as a reward. I learned that he was doing very well and totally enjoyed his job, so I left him in the job for the entire period.

When muzzleloader season arrived, I decided to do some serious scouting in preparation for the firearms period. It happened that he was supervising the assignment of hunting areas the afternoon that I chose to scout. When I told him what I wanted to do, he offered to allow me to use his black powder rifle - just in case I ran across a deer. I had never used such a weapon before, so he took the time to show me how to place the firing cap on the nipple and what to do with the triggers. Armed with the inside story on a promising area and a beautiful weapon, I entered the woods with anticipation.

I had hardly gotten started when I caught sight of a nice doe. She was heading my way along a fire trail that offered me a clear view from cover. What an opportunity! Maybe a buck would come along behind her. The doe turned off the trail a little over 50 yards out and began browsing. I watched her for about 20 minutes as she gradually worked her way through the open hardwoods feeding on acorns. I never saw a buck.

When I got back to the check station, I told my assistant game warden what had happened. "Why didn't you take her?" he asked. The question both surprised and disappointed me. "You should know that doe could only be shot during bow season" was my rather imperious reply. He chuckled, shook his head, and responded. "I wasn't implying that I would let you get away with poaching. Muzzleloaders are considered primitive weapons. It is entirely legal for you to shoot a doe with one."

I had not bothered to acquaint myself with the rules for black powder hunting. Not only had this mistake cost me a nice doe, I was both ignorant of the law, and stupid for not taking the few minutes needed to learn...and he knew it!

My oversight cost me a lot of embarrassment. Untold numbers of hunters rightfully pay a far heavier price each year in fines, lost weapons and vehicles, and revoked hunting privileges because they didn't bother to read and heed. Study the state regulations each year, even if you hunt in the same state every time. The rules change. Sometimes the changes are big, more often; they are subtle - but just as important. Either way, you, alone, are responsible to know and follow the laws. Keep them in your gear and reread them carefully before you venture out for each of the various seasons. Then, follow them to the letter. You may not get more game from this effort, but you will not suffer unnecessarily either.

8

RELOAD

My current hunting partner, having just taken a very respectable ten point buck (163 pounds field dressed) from his stand the day before, invited me to use it. There were only two days left in black powder rifle season, and I had planned to hunt; just not from his stand, *obviously*. But, I hunt on his property, so I decided to humor him. I had rarely hunted from his stand. It is about 125 yards from his front porch and in clear view of his house. His lawn and an un-mowed, grass meadow fill the space between.

His stand is a sturdy, four legged, metal tower that is ten feet high; and is six feet by six feet square at the top. We bolted a wood railing made from 2 by 4s around the top perimeter and attached a ground blind with a 75 inch high ceiling to the railing. Carpet covered plywood lies on the steel mesh floor to minimize noise and wind. The blind is equipped with a nicely padded swivel chair and a small, propane space heater (for those extra brisk days). It is a very comfortable perch that offers a great field of view in every direction. He calls it the "penthouse."

Help me describe the panorama from the stand for you. Close your eyes. Imagine that you are looking at a round, clock face (none of that digital stuff). Now visualize his house at 12 o'clock. The view from the stand, looking toward his house, is meadow from ten o'clock to three o'clock. Mature hardwoods occupy the area from three to nine. A ten feet high dirt berm borders the woods for about 40 feet at nine o'clock; then more meadow to nine forty-five. A rectangular grove of pine trees (20 yards house to stand by 70 yards) fills the space from nine forty-five to ten. A twenty acre crop field borders the entire property on the three o'clock side; about 80 yards distant from the stand at the closest point.

I had been scanning the woodlot from well before sunrise until about eight-thirty; periodically sweeping my view through 360 degrees on ten minute intervals. As my observation swung through the meadow near the tree line, I saw a large ten point buck standing broadside barely 20 yards away; looking into the woods less than ten yards distant from his nose. I raised my weapon, fired and dropped him flat. This startled me a bit because I was aiming low on his chest. While I was recovering from my surprise, he rose on his front legs and started to drag himself to the trees. His dramatically feeble efforts told me that I had no concern about him escaping; so I adjusted my focus to study the area where he was headed.

That was when I saw the doe. She came out of the brush on the tree line and watched his strange antics. I remember clearly thinking, she must be in estrus to be attracted to him so. I had two tags that I could fill. Belatedly, I started to reload my smoke pole. As fate, or more likely Murphy's Law, would have it, she stepped back into the trees; and I lost my chance for a clear shot at her. She circled a short distance in the woods for about ten minutes; continuously looking back toward the buck. I got fleeting glances through thick cover; but never had a shooting opportunity.

An hour after I was convinced the doe had left the area, I dismounted the stand and tagged my buck. When I field dressed him (198 pounds) I discovered that my shot had struck him where I wanted - a heart and lung shot - but as the slug passed through his ribs, a fragment of the bullet casing had broken away and cut his spinal cord. Sabots are devastating.

My only previous hunt from that stand (two years prior) had yielded a mature doe - and another incident of not reloading immediately after I fired - that time with my crossbow.

It was late in the afternoon, but not quite sundown. I was watching the tree line and into the woods as far as I could see when movement at the far left edge of my peripheral vision caught my attention. I slowly turned my head and saw a large doe leading five others toward me across the harvested soybean field. I immediately chose her as my target; pivoted 90 degrees, checked my crossbow, raised it to rest on the wooden rail around the tower stand and waited.

The deer came on at a steady pace and were soon entering the meadow that bordered the woods. The lead doe chose a trail that cut through the near center of the field before me and the others followed in trail. She had, apparently, decided to bed in the pine thicket that was now on my left as I faced towards my buddy's house (130+ yards away). She slowed as she followed the meandering path through the tall grass. I fired as she came broadside at 35 yards.

She recoiled as if startled when the bolt struck her. She hesitated a few seconds, then reversed direction and stumbled back toward the field. The other does reacted to her strange behavior by dispersing slightly and nervously avoiding her while studying her movements. She never ran, kept her tail clamped tightly down and collapsed just before she reached the border of the field and the meadow. Her fall triggered the other does to scatter in panic; but only a short distance. They soon stopped and milled about watching her feeble attempts to rise. When she lay still, all of the other does, save one, trotted away into the pine thicket.

Meanwhile, as I sat and observed the drama play out before me, I happened to notice a buck emerge from the tree line on the far side of the field. When he had walked only a few yards into the field, he stopped, watched the activities for a brief while, and then hurried back into the woods he had just left. I had no idea that the buck was anywhere in the area. It was early October, weeks before the rut, and none of the does had given any hint of being followed. They may not have known that he was there, either.

One doe remained in the field, circling her fallen matron. It finally dawned on me that I had a chance to take her; and, belatedly, began to re-cock my crossbow, which cannot be done by hand. I cranked the charging handle as fast as I could without moving a lot; got it ready, seated a bolt and raised it just as the doe walked into the tree line, now to my rear that I had been watching before the does came across the field. This last doe stayed in the trees for a short while, and then it appeared that she decided to rejoin the other does in the pine thicket. I could catch glimpses of her as she moved through the woods in that general direction, but I never got a shooting opportunity.

When I was very young; and carried a single shot shotgun, I remember having the reflexive habit of immediately reloading every time I took a shot. I got out of that habit when I "upgraded" to pump, then auto loading weapons. Now, I find myself foolishly watching deer walk away while I sit with an "empty" single shot weapon and observe.

Maybe there is a lesson here for everyone. I cannot begin to count the number of times that I have heard five rapid shots ring out in the woods during deer season. I know from personal experience that no one (except Jerry Mikulek) could possibly have held those shots on target. Hunters with multi-shot weapons "spray and pray;" and tend to miss as a result.

I know that I focus far more intently on executing the whole aiming process properly when I use my black powder rifle than I do with my shotgun or even my bolt action rifle. From observation and personal experience, (and I know it sounds counter-intuitive, but) I have come to the opinion that the vast majority of hunters would have far greater success when deer hunting if they had only one shot at their quarry. Single shot shotguns are the secret weapons for killing deer.

9

SOMETIMES YOUR GEAR FAILS YOU

MAKE SURE THAT YOUR GAME TRACKER IS STRUNG PROPERLY

I t had been stifling hot all day. The wind was light, and every mosquito and black fly in that South Carolina swamp had been dining on me for hours. I sat about 20 yards off a promising trail, my bow cradled in my lap. Finally, as the last rays of sunset pierced my eyes, a large doe came sidling along, nibbling on plants that edged the path.

Stiff from my long sit, I rose slowly, feeling awkward as my cramped muscles stretched in a jerky motion like gears with teeth missing. She did not notice my movements as I brought the compound to a full draw. Resting the 30-yard pin on her chest just back of her left shoulder, I felt very confident as I released the string.

The arrow fluttered out about 15 yards, trailing both ends of the bright orange dental floss like string that filled my deer tracker device, before crashing into the dry leaves.

The string made a sound a lot like a child makes when blowing air through loosely closed lips.

Instantly alert, the doe stood, poised for flight, and looked down that string, following it back to me. I stood transfixed, bow at arm's length, afraid to even blink my eyes, but it made no difference. When the line brought her focus onto me, she snorted so loud that I jumped, then she fled up her back trail in high loping bounds, flag erect.

When I retrieved my arrow (it was very easy to find), I discovered that I had apparently attached the wrong end of the line to the broad head. Only about six feet of line had left the tracker device when the other end became tangled and un-raveled as well. I was an experienced bow hunter who had neglected to practice with a new piece of equipment. It was a costly mistake.

WATCH FOR SLEET ON LONG ARM GUARDS

Opening day of bow season was unusually miserable. A stiff wind had been driving sleet into my face for over three hours. It coated me from head to foot in a frigid cocoon. I was about to give up when he came over the crest of the gently sloping pasture. It was the last place I expected, and the one spot that I had virtually ignored.

I was sitting on a stool among three large trees that formed a triangle. I leaned against the center tree; arms folded over the bow, and used the two immediately to each side to help hide me from view. Before me stretched hardwoods dropping left to right on a gentle slope. To my left was the pasture with a 20 by 30 feet patch of blackberry briars at its base. On my side of the patch, a very large tree had fallen, creating a natural blind. The big 14-pointer skirted the briars; casually jumped the three foot thick trunk of the fallen tree, and lay down.

My pulse was racing and I had trouble controlling my breathing! The largest buck that I had ever seen during bow season was just twenty-five or so yards from me.

I was so startled by his appearance - and size - that I had neglected to stand and draw my bow as he skirted the briars. After watching him for about a half-hour, I lost patience for sitting and waiting to see if he would leave his bed. I decided to try to walk up on him, at least far enough to clear the tree limbs between us. During the previous season, I had sat in the very spot he was now using and knew that his field of view was limited. The wind was causing a lot of movement, so I figured that I had a fair chance.

Ever so slowly, I stood and raised my bow in front of me... and he rose too! Panic gripped me as he stared hard in my direction. Then he shook the sleet from himself and lay back down. I started forward, sliding the left foot a shoe length, then the right. In about five minutes, I was totally exposed on the trail I had been watching. I never felt as naked in my life as at that moment, when he stood and peered at me a second time. He seemed to sense my presence, but apparently could not actually see me clearly. He sank onto his bed a third time, and I waited for long minutes before daring to inch forward again. After about 15 of the longest minutes I have ever endured, I was about 10 yards from him, and just clear of the tree limbs on my left.

With a clear view of my quarry, I realized that my test had just begun. He was lying just back from the log, facing in my direction. How could I draw, aim, and release without causing him to bolt? He turned his head away from me to nibble at his right flank. As quickly and smoothly as possible, I drew and fired. My shot was answered almost instantly by a loud thump as the arrow buried itself in a tree limb 10 feet ahead and slightly to my left.

The buck whipped his head around. I clearly saw recognition come into his eyes as he truly saw me for the first time. He rose and bounded the tree in a single movement that left me awe struck. I watched the empty trail, down which he had fled, for several seconds before coming back to my senses. That is when I noticed my arm guard dangling by a single strap. The end that should have been attached above my left elbow was still bent at nearly a 90-degree angle, frozen there by the sleet that had soaked it all morning. It had caught my bowstring and deflected the flight of the arrow.

I was hunting on a military reservation that permitted hunting on weekends only, and wasn't drawn for that area the next day. I was not overly concerned because I thought the buck would stay away for several days after such a narrow escape. The following Saturday, I was at the check-in building early to ensure a good chance at the draw. While waiting, I mentioned the big buck that I had seen the previous weekend to the warden. He asked me what area I was hunting. When I told him, he gave me a wry smile and said that a 16 year old had killed a 14 pointer in that area the Sunday before. It was his first hunt!

EVEN THE LATEST AND GREATEST CAN MALFUNCTION

During the 2019 deer season, I was sitting beside my son in a ground blind we called the "Yurt" with the younger of my two grandsons sleeping at my feet and the older fidgeting in boredom by me opposite his dad. About 20 minutes after sundown, my son suddenly tensed. I took his clue and as the 12 point buck walked boldly out into the field about 30 yards away I prepared to raise my four year old, very expensive, reverse limb crossbow. He had seen the buck first, so I waited while he took aim with his newer and even more expensive reverse limb crossbow.

The battery in his scope had died, so he "best guessed" the range mark on his unlighted scope in the near darkness - and shot over the deer's back. Since it continued to strut into the large sunflower field, as if nothing had happened, I smugly raised my crossbow, took aim and attempted to fire. Nothing happened. I pulled the trigger several times - to no avail. We watched that old monster prance away; still utterly unaware of us. The teenage son of my son's other hunting partner killed that buck the following weekend in that same blind. We guessed the buck to be about seven years old from the condition of his teeth and the grey hair scattered around his face.

My son installed a fresh battery in his scope the following day; and experienced no further problems - yes he did kill a buck later in the season. He also jokingly threatened to never allow his other partner or his son to hunt from that blind again - for killing "his" deer.

Both my son and I inspected and tried to fire my crossbow the next day; but could not get it to function. I took it to the local dealer. He inspected it thoroughly; then tried and failed to fire the weapon. Then he re-cocked the weapon. That was something I had not done because to all appearances it was already cocked; and I did not want to damage the cocking mechanism by over stroking it. To our joint surprise, the crossbow fired after being re-cocked. For some unknown reason, the cocking mechanism had cycled the safety selector and set the string retaining prongs; but had not set the trigger interface - or something like that. Anyway, we fired several follow-on shots with no issues. I subsequently fired the crossbow a dozen times in preparation for the 2020 hunting season with no further issues.

I had an incident similar to what my son experienced with his lighted scope. My sight failure was with a red dot scope during gun season. When I looked through the sight on my 12 gauge, I had only blank glass between me and the deer about 25 yards away. I could clearly see the end of my shotgun's barrel, so had no problem with windage, but I had no means of judging elevation. None the less, I fired - and missed. I cannot say if the slug went high or low. I can say that I was more than a little disgusted, because I had installed a "fresh" battery and I had checked the sight less than 30 minutes earlier; at which time it was working fine. Maybe the cold had affected the battery's performance.

I had a different, but equally disappointing experience with my 20 gauge shotgun. In that case, I had installed a new sight on an old gun; and I had sighted it at 25 yards. When I took the weapon deer hunting, I shot high at ranges over 25 yards (like in over the deer's back and I missed a nice six point buck). After I missed and the deer ran off, I determined the problem with my sight by shooting at a knot on a tree from 25, 35 then 50 yards - and witnessed the shots striking sequentially and dramatically higher as I moved out to the greater ranges. Why that happened still has me stumped. I could understand the slug striking a couple inches higher, but not more than half a body height. Maybe the fact that I was wearing more clothing affected my aim by changing how I presented to the weapon. I have gone back to good old fashioned iron sights on my shotguns and experienced no further problems. I strongly recommend sighting red dot scopes at a variety of ranges before using them to hunt.

10

B.R.A.S.S.

I have been married for very nearly a half-century. During that time, I have learned that my wife and firearms have many things in common. They are unforgiving of neglect and abuse, can do far more harm than you might believe, and are never to be dealt with in a frivolous or unthinking manner. They need and demand a certain minimal amount of attention. They can be very unpredictable, and require competent handling, care and treatment. Dealing with either while under the influence of alcohol or drugs is a certain recipe for disaster; but the repercussions that come with firearms are always far more deadly. They are highly reliable, and will serve (she hates that word!) beyond your expectations for a lifetime. They have an intrinsic beauty and sensuality; and the more closely that you hold them to yourself, the more forgiving they become. It takes time, observation, practice, and contemplation to become thoroughly familiar with each. They should not be selected in haste or on a whim. I have specialized in one woman for nearly my entire adult life.

Any competent scientist will tell you that one subject does not make a proper study group; so I will leave to you the decision about applying the commentary on my wife to other women. I will confine my remaining remarks to firearms and hunting safety.

I have spent over 67 years in the field, hunting; and over 20 years on active duty in the United States Marine Corps. During that time, I have acquired a body of knowledge about the handling, care, and use of firearms that has allowed me to hunt safely and successfully. I know, I know, you have heard all of what follows before, but...

First, choose your weapon wisely. A firearm is a highly specialized machine that is designed for the sole purpose of discharging a projectile at a target with great force and a high degree of accuracy. Make sure that the one you select is the proper size and caliber for you and for the type of shooting in which you plan to engage. Then handle and study it until you are thoroughly familiar with the feel. Adopt the attitude that "This is _my_ weapon. There are many others like it, but this one is mine. I will make it a natural extension of my body in the field. I will take close care of it, so it will be ready to perform well when needed." Most importantly, you must practice, practice, practice marksmanship.

A very famous basketball coach is said to begin each new season by calling his team together and saying "This is a basketball." Many people do not understand why he would make such a patently obvious statement to experienced players, but he had a genius for producing winning teams through the constant repetition of properly executed basic skills. Similarly, the greatest disappointments in hunting come from missing those shots that you know you should have made.

Marksmanship is surprisingly technical, and takes a great deal of attention and serious effort to master. You've got to rehearse to the point that you get it right without thinking about what you are doing. This takes time, but most of your drill sessions can be done at home with an unloaded weapon. Practice in the positions that you will use in the field. If you use a stool, or a seat strapped to a tree, practice with it at home, then take it with you to a range and shoot while sitting. When you shoot while standing, you should use a rest, like a tree trunk or limb, or a shooting stick to help steady your aim. Wear the same clothing that you will wear when hunting.

The first process to examine is holding the weapon. Hold it firmly, but do not squeeze it so hard that your hands or fingers feel strained.

A straining grip is unnatural, and will cause involuntary muscle tremors that will be transmitted into the weapon, degrading your ability to aim accurately.

Trigger squeeze is an interruptible, controlled process. Trigger control is vital in producing an accurate shot. Any pressure on the trigger, however slight, to the side, up or down, applied during the squeeze, will be transmitted into the weapon and cause the shot to go wide, high, or low. The trigger must be moved straight to the rear smoothly, gradually and evenly until the weapon fires. This must be done without disturbing the various elements of aim. This is best accomplished by using the part of the index finger between the tip and first joint. The trigger finger should not touch the weapon's stock. The rest of the trigger hand must grip the small of the stock firmly enough to allow the index finger to overcome the weight of the trigger. Use the thumb to wrap the opposite side of the small of the stock and complete a nearly circular grip. Do not rest it along the stock parallel to the barrel, or over the rear of the gun where it might interfere with sighting or strike you in the face or eye when the weapon fires.

The Marines have taught the basic rules of this process for decades. When I served, they describe it by the acronym B.R.A.S.S.- Breathe, Relax, Aim, Slack, Squeeze; they may still today.

B. BREATHE

If you continue to breathe while trying to aim a weapon, you will notice that the front sight will rise and fall over the target, thus preventing an accurate shot. Take in a normal breath and let part of it back out. Hold that breath until you fire. If you feel the need to breathe again before the weapon goes off, stop squeezing on the trigger, take another breath, and hold it while you continue to squeeze. An animal is rarely a stationary target. You may have to track it with your sights for some time before getting the shot you want. Consciously thinking about controlling your breathing will help you to stay calm enough to make an accurate shot.

R. RELAX

If you are tense while trying to fire a weapon, your body will shake. That movement will be transmitted into the weapon, thus destroying any chance of shooting accurately. You must consciously relax your muscles while aiming to minimize your shaking motions. This is particularly important when your system is flooded with adrenaline, as is always the case when a deer or other quarry is in your sights. Learn to control your body by forcing yourself to calm down during a particularly exciting sporting event, movie or video game. Train yourself to stay sufficiently calm and emotionally detached to be aware of what is happening around you. Do not allow your concentration to narrow your focus so much that you lose situational awareness.

A. AIM

Aiming a weapon is a far more involved process than most people expect. It includes body posture, body alignment to the target, sight alignment, aiming point, and sight picture. Whether you are standing or sitting, erect posture is essential to quality marksmanship. Your back must be straight, your shoulders square, and your head erect. Align your body with your target so that if the muzzle of your gun is disturbed, the natural point of aim will fall back somewhere near the center of your aiming point. The aiming point is the specific spot on the target that you wish to hit. Do not make the mistake of looking at the deer while you are shooting. You cannot shoot at a deer and know that you are going to hit it, much less that you will hit it in a vital spot.

You must pick that vital spot (aiming point) on its body, put your front sight on that spot, and keep it there until the weapon fires. On a deer, that spot is low on the chest (about one-third the vertical height of the chest) just behind the front leg.

Most shots taken while hunting are from the standing position. In that position, your body should be aligned to the animal's target area so that an imaginary line drawn from toe to toe of your boots would extend straight out and strike the center of your aiming point on the quarry. Golfers align themselves in a similar fashion before taking a swing at the ball.

When deer hunting, pick a couple spots along the trail you are watching that you would most like to catch a deer crossing, and establish feet positions for each. When the deer comes along, select the crossing you will use for the shot, set your feet in position, raise your weapon, aim in, track the deer in your sights, and fire as the deer crosses the spot.

You must place your gun in your shoulder correctly. It should line up with the stock parallel with your body and perpendicular to the ground plane, and should lie against your face. Squeeze your shoulder into your neck to bring the weapon up snugly against your face, and pull both arms back to your body to press the weapon firmly into your shoulder. Think about the spot where your face and the stock touch. This is the spot weld; the natural lay of the stock on your face and/or neck. It should be the same for a given shooting position each time that you prepare to aim from that position.

Sight alignment is the process of centering the tip of the front sight both horizontally and vertically in the rear sight. The eye cannot focus on two objects at different distances at the same time. To ensure proper sight alignment, hence a good shot, the eye must be focused on the tip of the front sight at the time that the weapon fires. Since the target cannot be ignored, you must first focus on the tip of the front sight and center it in the rear sight. Then shift your focus to the target and establish an aiming point. Finally, shift your focus back to the tip of the front sight and keep it there, while squeezing the trigger, until the weapon fires.

S. SLACK

Every trigger will move a short distance to the rear before your finger encounters resistance. This free movement is trigger slack. Learn to take up the slack in the trigger before starting to squeeze. This will reduce the tendency to jerk the trigger when shooting.

S. SQUEEZE

Squeezing a trigger means that you are in control of the force and direction in which the trigger is moved. Pull the trigger with a firm, steadily increasing, controlled pressure to the rear. Use only the tip of your index finger. Do not lay the first finger joint on the trigger, because you will pull the sights off target as you put pressure on the trigger. If your target moves into a position that is not favorable, hold the pressure on the trigger until it re-emerges, then resume the increasing pressure. At some point during this process, the weapon will fire. The discharge should come more or less as a surprise, but you should always know where the front sight is located at the time that it occurs.

You probably will not be consciously thinking about body position, breath and trigger control, firing lanes and B.R.A.S.S. when that big buck is walking along out in front of your stand. But, if you don't get them right, he will likely live to walk in front of someone else.

Practice, practice, practice in the off-season. Make these actions a natural part of your shooting, and you will dramatically improve your chances of taking that deer (or other game) home.

There is another vital reason that you must be able to control your weapon without conscious thought. You are obligated to know that the area through which your shot will travel to the target and the areas around and beyond where you intend your shot to strike are clear of other hunters, domestic animals, vehicles, and other items of personal property that people would not want damaged. This is most difficult to do when you are at the point of firing your weapon. Nevertheless, you have that responsibility. Thoroughly study the area where you expect your shot to fall well before any game appears. Take note of anything that your shot could place in danger. Shift (rotate) your position and choose new shooting lanes or relocate, if necessary, to avoid causing a hazard. Remain watchful. Hardest of all, you must remain sufficiently detached from your situation and in control of your faculties to be able to detect a hunter or other hazard that suddenly appears while you are aiming at your quarry, and hold your shot. There are no excuses for failing to practice shooting safety.

The above applies equally to all "long arms," by that I mean rifles, shotguns and crossbows. Pistol shooting requires the application of B.R.A.S.S., but demands much more attention to each facet to be performed well. The fundamentals of pistol marksmanship are aiming, trigger control, and breath control. This is far more critical than with long guns because of the short distance between the pistol sights. When shooting a pistol, a small error in sight alignment causes a considerable error at the target - a miss.

Breathing causes movement of the chest, abdomen, and shoulders, which causes the pistol sights to move vertically while attempting to aim and fire. Therefore, it is necessary to stop breathing for a period of time while firing a shot or a series of shots. The object of breath control is to stop breathing just long enough to fire the shot while maintaining sight alignment, stabilizing the sights, and establishing the sight picture

The grip is the key to acquiring sight alignment. To establish the grip, wrap your hand around the pistol in a manner that allows the trigger finger to move the trigger straight to the rear while maintaining sight alignment. There must be enough controlled muscular tension in your hands, wrists, and forearms to hold the pistol steady and level the barrel to your target while maintaining suitable sight alignment. If the grip is correct, the front and rear sights will align pretty much naturally. A firm grip is also essential for adequate trigger control. The pressure applied to the grip must be equal to or more than the pressure required to move the trigger to the rear without disturbing sight alignment to your target.

The human eye can focus clearly on only one object at a time. You must focus on the top edge of the front sight and fire the shot while maintaining the relationship between the front and rear sights within the aiming area. Focusing on the top edge of the front sight rather than the target keeps the front sight clear and distinct, which allows you to detect minor variations in sight alignment. You will see the target (although slightly blurred) well enough to maintain a proper sight picture within your aiming area.

Sight alignment and trigger control must be performed simultaneously to fire an accurate shot. Sight alignment is the relationship between the front sight and rear sight with respect to the aiming eye. Correct sight alignment is the front sight centered in the rear sight notch with the top edge of the front sight level aligned with the top edge of the rear sight. There should be equal space on either side of the front sight.

Sight picture is the placement of the front sight in relation to the target while maintaining sight alignment. You cannot hold a pistol totally still. Because the pistol is constantly moving, sight picture is acquired within the aiming area on the target. If you are deer hunting, the aiming area is the heart and lung area - basically the front one-half of the deer's chest cavity. Strive to keep the pistol aimed at a spot just behind the front leg about one-third up the height of the chest cavity. Your aim will drift around on the deer's chest. Do not let that fact bother you, as it is unavoidable. Just stay in the aiming area as near the ideal aim point as you are able. You define an acceptable aiming area by your own ability to stabilize the sights. As you practice, your aiming area will become smaller.

Trigger control is the manipulation of the trigger that causes the pistol to fire while maintaining sight alignment and sight picture. Squeezing a trigger means that you are in control of the force and direction in which the trigger is moved. Pull the trigger with a firm, steadily increasing, controlled pressure to the rear. Use only the tip of your index finger. Do not lay the first finger joint on the trigger, because you will pull the sights off target as you put pressure on the trigger. If your quarry moves into a position that is not favorable, hold the pressure on the trigger until it re-emerges, then resume the increasing pressure. At some point during this process, the weapon will fire. The discharge should come more or less as a surprise, but you should always know where the front sight is located at the time that it occurs. As pressure is applied to the trigger, the sights may move, causing them to be misaligned. To fire accurate shots, the sights must be aligned when the shot breaks. Trigger control can actually assist in aligning the sights. With proper trigger finger placement and consistent muscular tension applied to the grip, the sights can be controlled as the trigger is moved to the rear.

11

THE TREE STAND

A tree stand is one of the most useful items of equipment a deer hunter can own. It offers so many advantages over hunting on the ground that libraries of books have been written about it. The authors never seem to give many details on exactly how to set the thing up and use it, but every article that I have ever read includes at least a paragraph on safety precautions. Just in case you have not given much thought to rehearsing the set up and use of a stand or taken the safety instructions extremely seriously, I will share some of my earliest experiences with using one.

As deer season approached in 1977, my hunting partner bought a climbing tree stand. Since neither of us had ever used one before, we practiced attaching it to a tree in his yard and climbing. He took to the stand like he was born for it. I am not nearly as coordinated as he, so I had problems getting up and down the tree. I did not like bear hugging the tree, and I felt uneasy standing on a small platform at any height more than 12 feet off the ground. On opening day of his first season with it, he took a nice six-point buck at about 130 yards with his rifle. I hunted hard on the ground, and came up with an empty tag that year.

In spite of my initial experience, I decided to practice more with the stand between seasons, with an eye to getting a climbing stand of my own. I never seemed to get any better, so I decided not to buy one after all. Since he would not be able to hunt during the first part of the season, my hunting partner lent me his stand. On opening day of the 1978 season, I was in the woods well before sunrise. I hooked the stand to what I thought was the tree that I had selected during the preseason scout, and started my climb. Things went wrong from the start. I had not practiced in the heavy clothing that I was wearing to ward off the cold. I could not raise my legs more than a few inches at a time. I soon began to sweat from the effort.

Since I was making some progress, I persevered. About eight feet up, I ran into a large limb, and learned that I had chosen the wrong tree. Blocked, I worked myself down the tree and moved the stand to another that looked okay in the beam of my flashlight. I had again chosen poorly, and could not get a solid bite in the bark, which kept chipping away each time I put my weight on the stand. Thoroughly disgusted, I anchored the stand about two feet off the ground and used it as a seat.

I had gotten so wet from sweating that I was thoroughly chilled by 9:00 am. Since I had seen nothing and heard few shots, I gave up the morning hunt as a bad effort. I left the stand in place for the afternoon hunt and hiked out for lunch. When I got back to my truck, I noticed several others had gathered around their trucks a short distance away. Like most other hunters, I went over to inquire if they had gotten a deer or seen any. I did not expect the reply. They were standing around talking about the fool who had made so much noise with his tree stand for so long that they had given up. As I was too embarrassed to confess that I was the culprit, I played along until I could find a way out of the conversation that I had started.

My hunting partner got back just before the end of the season. We got in one hunt. It turned out to be one of my most memorable. He set up his tree stand overlooking a long meadow. I took a ground stand about 50 yards away, on the backside of a steep hill with a good view of a valley. We stayed on stand until well past lunchtime. We met around 1:30 pm, ate and sat around camp discussing the prospects for the rest of the day.

While we were sitting there, an old hound dog came by and timidly, tail tucked between rail thin legs, invited himself into our company. He looked so haggard and foot sore that we couldn't bring ourselves to drive him away. We kept some C rations in our hunting gear as emergency food stores in case something happened to keep us out all night. We decided to use them to feed the dog. He ravenously ate everything we offered. That is, until we gave him the chocolate. It had the shape and consistency of an old hockey puck. I still chuckle with the memory of watching him take the disk, bite, give us the most disappointed look I have ever seen on a dog's face, and proceed to bury it. Really! I have since learned that chocolate is very bad for dogs. Maybe he was smarter than I.

Anyway, during the afternoon the heat climbed and the wind picked up. I didn't give us much hope for the afternoon portion of the hunt. My partner was anxious to stay because this would be, virtually, our only opportunity for the rest of the season. We went back on stand. I was reluctant. For some reason that totally eluded me, he seemed anxious.

I neither saw nor heard anything until just at sunset, when the report from his rifle startled me. The heavy thud and thrashing noise that followed almost immediately worried me. I rushed over to his stand and found it still attached to the tree about 15 feet off the ground. My search of the thick growth of brush near the stand yielded no sign of him. I was thoroughly frightened, and nearly jumped out of my skin when he yelled from across the meadow.

I ran over to find that he had shot a buck that was even larger than the one he had gotten the year before. He was more exhilarated than I had ever seen him. His elation evaporated quickly; however, when I managed to get his attention well enough to ask him how he had gotten out of his stand. "Stand? Stand? Oh sh_t! I saw the buck go down and came running over to see if he was really as big as he had looked in my scope." he sputtered as he gazed, wide eyed, across the meadow to his stand, which was still perched in the tree.

In his excitement, he had forgotten where he was and walked out of the stand. Fortunately, he suffered no more than some badly strained muscles. We spent nearly an hour coaxing that thing out of the tree, with a long pole fashioned from a sapling. The whole experience left me a devoted ground hunter for many years.

The stand had seemed to be such a simple piece of equipment that we had approached learning to use it in a complacent manner. We were doubly lucky during these experiences. First, no one had gotten seriously hurt.

Secondly, the fact that we desperately needed extensive practice in using the stand safely came home to us in a graphically personal way.

So that is the "Why" of tree stands safety. Here are some ideas of the "How" of tree stand safety.

Read and follow the instructions... Every tree stand comes with instructions outlining assembly and proper use. After you have thoroughly read the information, keep the paperwork! Review the instructions at least every year - and pass them along if you sell your tree stand.

Wear the clothing that you will use to hunt and practice, practice, practice until you perfect your climbing routine in the preseason; especially if you are using a climber-style tree stand. The more you sweat in the preseason, the less likely you are to bleed from injuries in the hunting season. Developing that muscle memory is very important to help make you safer when you climb for a hunt. When practicing, it is best to climb just a few feet from the ground (no more than six to eight feet); and to have a friend nearby who can help you if you run into a problem.

None of us want to think about the possible consequences of a fall from a tree stand. However, failing to prepare for this scenario may leave you in a critical situation. **Always Wear A Full-Body Fall Arrest Harness System** (FBFAHS); and **only** use a Tree stand Manufacturer's Association approved FBFAHS. Educate yourself on the proper way to put your FBFAHS on, how to properly secure it to a tree, and how to adjust it after the climb for sitting in your stand.

The FBFAHS works by distributing the fall arresting forces safely over your upper and lower body and it allows you to be freer in your movement while using your hunting equipment. Do not go cheap! Partial body harnesses, like those that only cover the chest or go around the waist, should **NEVER** be used as tree stand safety harnesses because they are not designed to evenly distribute the arrest forces that result from the fall over the trunk of your body. Using a partial body harness can lead to serious injury or even death if you experience a fall.

These systems are offered in a range of weight ratings up to 350 pounds. Purchase the FBFAHS that is appropriate for your weight. Your weight is the combination of your personal weight and the weight of the clothing and equipment that you are wearing and carrying while on stand. Always use an FBFAHS that is rated for slightly, but not grossly, more than your weight. If you are too heavy for the FBFAHS you currently own, buy a higher rated FBFAHS or do not hunt from a tree stand.

Your FBFAHS is designed to keep you safe in the event of a fall; but, even if your FBFAHS functions properly, hanging for several hours can cause serious long-term physical problems or even death to any hunter, regardless of age and physical condition. After falling, first attempt to recover and climb back on to your stand. If this is not possible, call for help immediately.

If you must hang for an extended period, move your legs and arms by pushing against the tree or by some other method. This leg and arm movement helps to promote continuous blood flow throughout your body and helps to prevent possible cardiac arrest.

Lanyards and fall arrest systems are available for use in conjunction with a FBFAHS; but you must be very careful to ensure that if you choose and use one it is of appropriate length to function before you hit the ground. The length varies by devise. You must know with certainty how high you will consistently be off the ground to select the correct devise.

A Hunter Safety System "Lifeline," which is rated up to 400 pounds is available and very reasonable priced, as of 2020. It engages very quickly after a fall and allows the user to descend by means of a rope and "block and tackle" type of device completely to ground level.

Do not discount Murphy's Law. Always keep a knife or cutting tool ready and available to you (within reach while hanging) should you fall.

If you cannot climb back onto the stand, or the fall arresting system fails and you are unable to contact help that will respond within less than two hours, then use the knife or cutting tool to cut the safety lanyard above your head and drop to the ground. This is a last resort option, but far better than cardiac arrest.

A critical reason to scout and mark tree stand locations on a map in the preseason is that you should always choose a tree that best fits the tree stand manufacturer's recommended dimensions. Do not use trees that are dead, unhealthy, crooked, excessively knotted, or that lean; and do not put a stand up near a tree that is dead or unhealthy. Be sure to clear debris from around the base of the tree to minimize your injuries if you fall. Do not leave the stand in the woods longer than your stand maker recommends.

At ALL times possible, hunt with a buddy who can help out if an emergency arises. If you must hunt alone, notify a reliable person of your exact hunting location. Provide that person with a detailed map (a copy of the map you create during the preseason hunt site scout), so rescuers can find you quickly. Better yet, take your contact person with you when scouting hunt sites in the preseason (and marking site choices on the map) so that person will know your sites and can lead rescuers. Notify this person every time you are going to the woods and when you expect to leave the woods. Also inform this person when you are safely out of the woods.

It is never a good idea to try to rush into or out of your stand - there is no sense in breaking an ankle or leg, or getting blinded by a twig in the eye while moving to or from your stand site. When you rush, you cannot focus completely on the task at hand, and you are opening yourself up to the possibility of an accident. When you climb, be sure that you make slow, even movements and that you stay in proper contact with the tree and/or tree stand with each movement. If you hunt from a ladder stand or an elevated blind with steps and a railing, you should have two hands and one foot or one hand and two feet in contact with the ladder or stairs and railing at all times.

Like Clint Eastwood says, "A man's got to know his limitations." Always know your physical limitations and do not push yourself past them. If you are tired, sleepy or for any other reason do not feel alert **do not climb**; have a back-up hunting plan in place and use a different hunting set up for that day. If you are using a climbing stand and you feel like you are high enough, stop climbing. Sometimes "high enough" is seated on the climbing stand with your feet on the ground. After I had back surgery, I switched from a climbing tree stand to a ladder stand. It was more expensive to erect several ladder stands at various locations, but I was able to keep hunting.

The ability to draw attention to your location means that rescuers will be able to pinpoint your exact location more quickly.

Carry communication **and** emergency signal devices like a cell phone, flashlight, flare, and whistle. Having a device that will emit a signal without your attention (flashlight or flare) would be critical if you lose consciousness. It might mean the difference between your life and death. Keep these devices on your person in a place where they are unlikely to get broken if you fall; yet are easy to reach if you are lying on the ground. Confused? While you are home, dress in the clothing you will wear when hunting, then lie on the ground and put these devices in your available pockets - use the same pockets when you hunt.

Finally, never climb a tree with your climbing stand or go up your ladder into your stand with objects in your hands or on your back. Always use a hoist rope to raise your weapon, pack, and any other equipment you need into the stand **after** you have secured your FBFAHS to the tree. Be sure to lower your equipment to a location on the ground that does not interfere with your exit route down the tree, ladder, or stairs before leaving your elevated stand.

AND MAKE CERTAIN THAT YOUR WEAPON IS NOT LOADED BEFORE RAISING OR LOWERING IT FROM YOUR STAND!!

When shooting from any vertical position relative to your prey, you must contend with old Pythagoras and his immutable Theorem. There is a mathematical formula that you can use to derive exactly how high you will hit when taking angled shots or how low you will hit when shooting straight down. Do you remember from your high school days (daze) that "A" squared plus "B" squared equals "C" squared? Forget that when you are in an elevated position and you will miss your shot! It applies to hunting in the following way: "A" is the height of your stand relative to the deer. "B" is the horizontal distance along flat ground from your position to the deer. "C" is the diagonal distance from your position to the deer. These are the two distances that you need to take into account if you want to get an accurate shot.

Shooting uphill, downhill, or at a downward angle from a tree stand causes the point of impact to be higher than if you had taken the shot from the same distance on level ground. The closer the animal is to you when you take the shot, the steeper the downward shooting angle is from your elevated position to the animal. The steeper the downward angle, the shorter the horizontal distance is that the projectile travels; and the higher your point of impact will be. However, when an animal is directly beneath you (or very nearly so) your point-of-impact will be low.

One effective method for you to use to determine the correct range is to use your range finder while standing at the base of your tree or stand to measure the distance from your chosen shooting position to various trees near the trail that you expect the deer to follow. Select and mark a few trees in some fashion of your choosing that will indicate their horizontal distance to your shooting position. You might spray paint the yardage number on trees. I use colored tape.

Another way is to practice ranging and shooting out of your stand at a target set up at closer and longer distances. You should also practice shooting your target when it is positioned directly below you to determine the point of impact.

Using this approach, you can learn how much you will need to adjust your point of aim to hit a vital area with your shot, regardless of the animal's distance from you.

For those who hunt enough to invest both firearm and bow hunters alike can benefit from using rangefinders with angle compensation. Situations where they are helpful for include:

- Any hunter ranging in unknown territory; or in areas of steep terrain
- Archers using any type of bow (recurve, compound or crossbow) in an elevated blind
- Rifle hunters shooting extreme distances

DON'T BE IMPULSIVE

Yes, this actually happened - sometimes truth really is stranger than fiction. Deer season is one of those times when strange things occur and men have "Hey watch this" moments without stopping to say, "Hey watch this."

I know two hunters who used an old panel van as a hunting vehicle because it was so beaten up that they could do little more damage to it on their weekend deer safaris. On one particular morning, they got a late start.

Worried that they would not get into the woods before sunrise, they went hurtling down a graveled, country road. Suddenly, they saw hair, antlers and eyeballs rushing at them down the beam of the headlights. Unable to stop in time, they hit the buck hard, lost control of the vehicle, and came to rest in a shallow ditch.

Shaken, but unhurt, they inspected the van and decided that the damage, though extensive, was not serious enough to keep them from their hunt. They then turned their attention to the deer. He had been thrown several yards off of the road by the impact, and appeared to be dead. His left front side was bloody and he didn't appear to be breathing. Without checking to be certain, they threw him in the back of the van and continued on to camp.

They had not gone far when the van's owner began to worry about getting caught with a deer that had not been tagged. After a brief argument about who would sacrifice his tag, the passenger climbed into the back of the van, cut a slit in the buck's right front leg and attached the driver's deer tag. As he rose from his task, so did the buck. It caught him squarely between the tines of its antlers and shoved him all over the back of the van while he desperately clung to its neck. Fortunately for the man holding the buck, its left front shoulder and leg had been severely injured in the accident. It couldn't get both front feet squared under itself on the blood slick, metal floor.

The driver struggled to bring the van to an emergency stop on the loose gravel; all the while trying to see what was happening just behind him. At about the time that the van skidded to a stop, the deer and his companion hit the rear doors. The latch gave way and they tumbled onto the road. The man landed on his back, flipping the deer over himself onto its back just beyond him. The deer rose and tried to run, but kept falling. It crashed through some dense underbrush beside the road and disappeared. By now, the driver had leapt from his seat and rushed to the rear of the van. He found his friend lying on the road, moaning in a semiconscious condition. He had not been gored, but he had gotten two cracked ribs and many cuts and bruises.

Later that same day, after a quick trip to a local emergency room, they returned to the sight of the fracas. They found the buck lying about 40 yards from the roadside. This time he was most assuredly dead. The buck dressed out at 165 pounds. The man who had wrestled it mounted his head and rack. It hangs on his wall as a constant reminder of his narrow escape.

I shot a doe one afternoon, and watched her go down in a heap. I walked over to her, and saw a gash running across the top of her head almost exactly from ear to ear.

I also noticed that her eyes were closed. I backed up a few feet and watched her closely for several minutes. Seeing no sign of movement, I positioned myself behind her, as far from her hooves as I could get, and jabbed her hard in the back with my gun barrel. The effect was electrifying to her, and startling to me. In a flash, she was on her feet and running hard for cover. I was so flustered that I did not think to take a shot until she was out of sight. I never did find her again.

I had a somewhat similar incident with a young buck that I had shot with a bow. He was down with his eyes closed when I found him, but he rose in a rush when I stuck him in the rump with the point of an arrow. I tracked him for nearly half an hour before I found him again. When I finally did, I spent another arrow to make very certain that he would not get up anymore. From that time to this, I always take another shot if I have even the slightest doubt about whether a deer is alive or dead.

No matter what the circumstance or the apparent extent of a deer's injuries, never assume that it is dead. If its eyes are closed, chances are it is not dead. There is no guarantee that it is dead even if its eyes are open. Examine the animal thoroughly from a safe distance before moving up to check it closely from behind. Stay away from the hooves and antlers. If you are not absolutely certain that the animal is dead, take another, well placed shot to the lower rib cage just behind the front leg. The insurance shot does little damage to the meat. It can mean the difference between an easy recovery and a long search - or worse. You will have plenty of time to tag and dress your prize later.

Every year, I either read or listen to a news article covering a hunter's death, or the serious injury that he has sustained because he failed to practice my habit. When you drop a deer, particularly a large buck, your first impulse is normally to rush to it yelling for joy. This action can have harrowing, if not tragic consequences. In many ways, a deer is hide and hoof covering spring steel. Respect it.

13

THE BET

From 1982 through 1986, I had the pleasure of hunting in a virtual deer hunter's paradise. The place was a federal facility that was badly overpopulated in deer. The local authorities encouraged taking as many deer as possible from preselected areas with boundaries that, for safety and security reasons, each hunter could not leave. During the first four seasons, I took one buck each gun season and another along with two does during the bow seasons. I did not take more deer only because I chose not to buy more permits. So what? Well, I accomplished this small feat hunting only on opening days, and I never got home later than 2:00 pm. My wife began to think that deer hunting was like shopping!

In 1986, I started working with an immodest "nimrod" who, by his own declaration, was a deer hunter of some renown. He disputed my claims that such a hunting area could exist. He also doubted that I was skilled enough to consistently kill deer that readily. Since I have an ego of noteworthy proportions, I would not let his challenge go unanswered. I bet him a dollar - and bragging rights - that I could take a deer with a bow, and have it, field dressed, in the back of my vehicle by noon on opening day. He readily accepted, insisting that he would hunt with me to ensure that if I accomplished the task (a big if to him), I completed it honestly. I agreed.

By the way, did you ever wonder where the term nimrod came from? Webster's dictionary indicates that "Nimrod" originates in the Bible. There, he is described in Genesis as "the first on earth to be a mighty man" and "a mighty hunter before the Lord." It's easy to see how people made the leap from one mighty hunter in the Bible to calling any hunter a Nimrod. He is associated with the disastrous Tower of Babel. So the term "*nimrod*" is also used to mean: "a tyrant; a stupid person; an idiot; a jerk" when not capitalized.

My newly acquired hunting partner then told me about the one small problem to be overcome before we could play our little drama out. He did not know how to shoot a bow! During the few weeks we had before bow season opened, I found myself spending a lot of time teaching him basic archery techniques. I cannot really say if I was a poor instructor, or he was a slow student. Suffice to say that his skills were hard won. His progress is best described by his own admission that he shot no less than six times at a young doe that was standing broadside to him at about 30 yards; then had to chase her away to retrieve his arrows.

My hunting paradise was located on a military ammunition storage base. No one was allowed to actually scout. We chose adjoining hunting areas, both of which had produced well for me previously. I was so confident that I would get a good shot at a deer in either area that I described each to him, and gave him first choice. I took him to the stand where I had hunted in the area he selected, and rushed to my own spot.

The weather was glorious that morning. The sky was clear, the air was cool, the wind calm. The trees seemed to almost glow in the first rays of daylight. Very little rainfall in the days leading up to opening day meant that the leaves were dry and noisy. Nothing could go wrong... Sometime between 7:30 am and 10:00 am that morning, a deer would come down the well-worn trail I was watching, and I would win the bet.

At almost exactly 8:30 am, I heard the first faint noises. They were coming from the back of a small hill some 40 yards in front of me and slightly to my right. It was hard to pinpoint the source, but I knew that they had to be made by an animal moving toward me, yet slightly off the trail that I was watching. I hoped that it was a deer browsing for acorns in the open hardwoods.

I soon noticed a rounded shape rising slowly through the sparse underbrush as my quarry advanced up the rear slope. The glint of sunlight reflecting from the new broad head mounted to the tip of his arrow instantly identified the shape as the camouflaged head of my ersatz hunting partner. I had caught sight of him just a he started to raise his bow over his head. It was a very noticeable movement. I do not know why he did that, and, later, I forgot to ask.

I laid my bow back across my lap and sat quietly, steaming, as I watched him come on. I was hidden in a pile of large rocks, which formed a natural horseshoe shape. A tree with foliage growing down to about four feet over my head provided me shade, a backrest, and additional cover.

He never noticed me until I spoke to him as he passed by a few feet away. Obviously startled, for a few seconds he seemed at a loss for anything to say. Then he half smiled and said, "I haven't seen a thing. Did you get one yet?" It could have been the tone in his voice, but I think the smile is what caused me to remember his words so vividly.

He then mentioned something about how great my spot was and how he wished that he had chosen my area. I chewed on his words for a few seconds while I tried to decide how to solve my dilemma. "Since you're here, why don't we switch? I'll go back to your stand." It was the only thing I could think of to get him off my back! He agreed.

I left by the same route that I had come in to the stand; circled widely, and approached what had been his stand from a crosswind position. I didn't hold out much hope for success at that point, but I went on stand and waited.

An hour passed with hardly a bird or squirrel moving. When I heard slight noises coming toward me from behind, I half expected to turn and see him again. Still, there was just a chance that it would be a deer. I turned very slowly and saw a doe gradually working her way in my direction as she browsed.

I had gotten lucky. The doe presented me with a broadside shot at just over 30 yards. She jumped as I released the string. The arrow struck in her rib cage about six inches back from my aiming point. She looked at the shaft, then turned and trotted out of sight along her back trail.

There are two schools of thought about how long a hunter should wait before pursuing a wounded deer. Some professional bow hunters insist on waiting for an hour or more before following a deer to give it time to relax, lie down and die. Others contend that keeping the deer moving hastens its demise. I don't adhere strictly to either school.

First, I sit and stare at the spot where the animal was standing when I took my shot until I calm down. Then I thoroughly study every tree and landmark at that location. When I have a very clear idea of where I am going, I move to that spot. I never take my eyes off my destination for longer than is absolutely necessary to travel there without tripping or running into anything.

When I arrive, I locate some sign that I have hit the animal (usually blood, occasionally a tuft of hair; and, rarely, smelly, greenish-brown stomach or gut matter. *I never try to trail a stomach or gut shot deer until the next day after I shot it.*) and mark it with a square of unscented, white toilet paper. The paper is easy to see in the woods, and dissolves during the first rainfall. Following the path the deer took in flight; I mark every drop of blood or tuft of hair that I find with other sheets of paper.

If the trail goes dry, as this one did, I look back along the sequence of white squares and establish a line of movement in my mind's eye. I then turn in the reverse direction and pick a tree or other noticeable landmark further along that imaginary route. Having a good idea of where I should be headed, I get down on my hands and knees and proceed toward that point searching for new signs. Occasionally, I will stand and look back to make certain that I am still on my intended movement line, getting back on track if necessary. When I find the next sign of my quarry, I again mark it with a white square and proceed.

It was by this method that I located the partial shaft of my arrow. The doe had moved into some thick, low brush and broken it off in passing. This had reopened the wound in her side. The trail became much easier to follow for a good distance; so I stood and resumed tracking. When I broke out of the brush, I was overlooking a sloping meadow of high grass, and the trail gave out again. There were innumerable paths facing me, but it was a large open expanse with a road bordering the bottom. I was convinced that she was lying out there somewhere.

I studied that grass in my binoculars for at least a half hour before I noticed a small clump of grass that moved differently than the rest in the slight breeze. As I focused intently on that spot, her outline gradually appeared. Nocking a fresh arrow, I edged toward her. She rose, slowly, to flee when I was about ten yards away. This shot was better placed. She went back down almost immediately.

Then I got worried about the clock and the bet. She weighed only a little over 100 pounds, so the field dressing and dragging went quickly. We went downhill to the road together. I left her and hurried back to my vehicle. Fifteen or twenty minutes later, I stopped as close to the stand area where I had left my hunting partner as I could. With total disregard for his situation, I laid on the horn and yelled into the woods. He soon emerged. It was a little before twelve o'clock, and I was triumphantly elated. I did not bother to ask for "my" dollar... and he never volunteered it.

That was my last "good" season hunting in those areas. I transferred before the next season, and was gone for three years. When I returned, the deer seemed to have disappeared. Nothing had changed in the outward appearance of the areas, but the deer population had collapsed.

14

BE COURTEOUS

The morning seemed to drag on for weeks. The incessant wind sent low, gray clouds scudding south and kept the trees moaning. With the temperature hovering well below freezing, the damp air seemed to knife through clothing and flesh to send a chill cutting into the bones. I hadn't seen so much as a bird. I heard a few shots early, but none after about 8:00am. Around 11:00am, I decided that camp offered more rewards than my stand.

I was yards from the camper when I notice a hunter moving very slowly across the large meadow behind our campsite. From his stooped posture and erratic, stop-and-go progress I sensed that he was tracking a wounded deer. Tall grass and the spotty growth of young pine trees prevented a clear view of the area, but I knew from experience that deer moved through the center of the shallow valley that the meadow grew over and entered the hardwoods at its head. Normally, they then turned left toward a thick stand of pines that they regularly used as a bedding area. That bedding area was about 300 yards directly to my left, but almost a half-mile from the hunter by the deer trail he seemed to be following.

Dividing up and sharing venison is a decades old tradition that all of the hunters in the five camps in the area practice. If someone gets a deer, he shares with his hunting partners and with anyone who directly helps him get the deer, or get it out of the woods. That way, a hunter is reasonably sure to take some meat home even if he doesn't fill his own tag. It is a system that works to everyone's advantage because it gives an incentive to help each other track, dress and drag deer, and reduces squabbles over who a deer belongs to in situations where one wounds a deer and another kills it. If you are the guest of another hunter and you kill a deer, you should offer your host first choice of meat cuts.

With this in mind, I hurried along my side of the meadow and took up a hasty stand thirty odd yards in the hardwoods. The wind was in my favor, and I told myself that he must have hit the deer over three hours ago so it should be moving slow and lying down often by now. I was right! I saw the doe a scant five minutes after I arrived. She got up from the brush that grew at the border of the meadow and the hardwoods, and started my way. Still over 150 yards away, I could not see where she was wounded, but could readily tell that she was badly injured. She went down into a small gully and disappeared. Long minutes passed as I searched every possible direction that she could have gone. Suddenly, she burst into view about 70 yards away on the trail that I was watching. At about 50 yards, I could clearly see that she had been hit low, several inches behind her rib cage. With my doe permit safely tucked in my breast pocket, I let her come on until she was broadside to me. I put her out of her misery.

My single shot was answered by "Hey, did you shoot my deer?" yelled from my right. The deer down, I turned to watch the hunter rushing in my direction. As he got closer, I recognized him. His camp was close to ours and we had occasionally visited over the years. "Hit a button buck early. Been pushing' him ever since," he gasped as he neared me. "Button buck?" I asked.

"Well, yeah, at first I thought he was a spike, but he was on me so fast that I never got a good look. After he went down, I started for him, but then he got up and took off. That's when I realized he must be a button, 'because I couldn't see antlers."

He had made a poor shot, but he had persisted while tracking her, so I replied, "Got a doe permit?" "Sure, why?" he said. "Because, your doe is over there." I said, nodding in the direction of where she lay. "Doe?" he said, disappointed, then "Where? I don't see her." I led him the few yards to where she lay. He tagged her and then started fumbling in his pockets. Looking a bit sheepish, he said "Left my stuff on the ATV. Mind keeping an eye on her until I get back? I shouldn't be long." I agreed to wait and watch over the doe's carcass for him...

He had been gone for quite some time when I decided to go ahead and field dress the doe. Still, I had been finished for a while before I heard the ATV coming. When he pulled up, I lifted the doe onto the carrier and we tied her down. "Thanks. Here's a shell to replace the one you used" he said, proffering a 12-gauge slug. Taken aback, "I use a 20." was all I could think to say. He shrugged, put the shell back in his pocket, and left.

I was still angry when I got back to camp. This guy had not offered me even so much as a shoulder for doing literally everything for him! We had shared out with him for using his ATV to get a deer out of deep woods two years past. He knew our agreement, and he broke it. When word got around the other camps, even his own hunting partners were disgusted with him. I got a personal apology from one of them, representing, he said, the group. I received no venison. I never saw the offending hunter again. If the opportunity ever presents itself in the future, I will send the hunter into the thick growth pines and keep the deer, which I should have done the first time, because I had killed the deer.

Everyone knows that he (or she) is expected to understand hunting regulations; and abide by them. Those regulations are established by legal statutes passed by legislatures and enforced by officers of a court. But we too often forget that there are also unwritten laws of habit and mutual expectation - the common laws that govern hunters; those are generally understood, but not openly spoken.

When you are in a wilderness or near wilderness location; a forestry area with which you are not entirely familiar or terrain that is challenging to traverse and from which removing a deer carcass is exhausting as applicable examples, you are or can easily become dependent on the good will and cooperativeness of others. Your best interest dictates that you conduct yourself in a friendly and courteous manner.

Common law in general society is defined as law that is derived from custom and precedent rather than legal statutes. When someone hunts with or around others, whether those "others" are integral to the core group or not, a set of expectations concerning hunting conduct in the field gradually develop - just like "common law" in everyday society. A hunter who fails to heed and follow the common laws of etiquette established by the group with whom or near whom he (or she) hunts will, most assuredly, find himself (herself) facing difficulties in the field - and receiving grudging, if any, assistance. He (she) may well even find himself (herself) facing difficulties that would never have arisen had he (she) been considerate enough to learn and abide by the rules of courtesy established by the local group.

15

IRONY ON OPENING DAY

Hunting has always been a quest only suited for the determined and stout hearted. It requires patience, perseverance, exertion, and the capacity to handle disappointment. November mornings sometimes seem to have been created solely for sitting in the woods breathing frigid air, absorbing the beauty of the surroundings, and tingling with anticipation. This morning was for me. The cloudless sky was a beautiful azure. Frost made the black skeletons of the leafless trees glisten in the golden rays of the rising sun.

I had only been hunting whitetails for a couple seasons, but I had scouted the area thoroughly, and knew my stand was well placed. At various times since first light, shots rang out from different locations around me. I seemed to be in the very center of all the activity.

My excitement roused, I watched and listened anxiously. Still, I was not truly prepared for the sudden appearance of a virtual herd of deer. They bounded in so silently that they seemed to materialize from the crisp air.

Two large does sandwiched three smaller ones. A four-point buck was in trail, but so close that I got the impression that he would have been in the midst of the group if the older does had allowed him to be. He acted so timid that I did not realize that a buck was there for several seconds.

They stopped scant yards from where I sat hidden. Obviously undecided about what to do next, the lead doe started off to my right, froze, then reversed and stopped again. The others milled about, pawing and watching her for guidance. This stationary group, that was at once a beehive of activity, transfixed me. Their heads jerked from side to side while their ears swiveled in different directions simultaneously. One doe raised its tail almost fully vertical then snapped it back down hard between its haunches. The hair rose along another's back while its flanks shivered.

Watching this scene, the hair rose on the back of my neck, my heart began to pound, and I had to force myself to be calm and think about how I could take advantage of the moment. I must have moved, because one of the young does locked her eyes on me in a gaze of total panic. Then almost immediately, she snorted loudly, stamped her right front hoof, and launched over another's back in a mad dash into the open woods. The second large doe and the doe that had been jumped followed immediately. The first doe, her daughter, and the buck remained. Tense as coiled springs, they turned their gazes away from me and watched the others rapidly disappear in long leaps.

I had my chance. Raising the gun to my shoulder in a motion honed by many shots at quail, I stood and brought the bead onto the buck's chest. Almost simultaneously, I disengaged the safety with my trigger finger. The metallic click was electrifying. The lead doe spun completely around and bounded down the trail. The yearling doe nearly ran under her as it followed. The buck went straight down, and then turned in the opposite direction the last doe had taken, and fled down his back trail. His initial move fooled me. I shot over his back. I chambered a new shell as I tracked him briefly with my gun barrel, and then fired again. He crumpled.

The adrenalin surging in me caused me to work the pump mechanism and fire again faster than I had ever thought possible. My third, and last, shot ripped through the air above him before I actually realized that he had collapsed. He rose and tottered drunkenly away as I fumbled in my coat for more shells. By the time that I managed to reload, I was shaking so badly that I nearly dropped my gun. I sat back on my stool, thankful for the tree that kept me from toppling over backwards. Long minutes dragged by before I trusted myself to rise and start looking for sign.

When I did, I soon found the large, bloody spot in the leaves where he had gone down. Confident that I would find him a short distance away, I gathered my gear and started tracking. I worked my way along the trail as it ran along a hillside. Little more than 50 yards from where he had fallen, I lost all sign of him. I realized only then that I should have taken the time to mark the trail as I proceeded.

Leaving my stool to mark the point of my farthest progress, I returned to the spot where I had found the first blood sign and started laying squares of white toilet paper on every drop of blood that I found. I soon saw from that line of squares that his path of movement was taking him off the trail and back up the hill into the woods. Belatedly, I understood that the buck had circled behind me, as I sat leaning against the tree. I retrieved my stool and started tracking him again. Now, I was moving over ground that was more familiar. The slope flattened into a wide, shallow valley. The road on which I, and several others, had parked before sunrise that morning was only a hundred yards or so to my right.

In a few minutes, I found another area of disturbed, bloody leaves where he had apparently lain down again. No doubt, he had moved from there when I had gotten up to start tracking him. The buck's wound had reopened, making the tracking a lot easier. I was making good progress when the sharp clang of a tailgate slamming on one of the trucks startled me. I jumped involuntarily, and then froze. A couple of seconds later, the door banged shut and the engine fired. I heard the gravel pop under the tires as the driver launched the truck onto the narrow road and tore off.

I stood like a statue and watched intently to see if the buck would be frightened from his hiding place by the noise. The sounds quickly faded and he did not move. I returned to my task, working steadily over the flat ground. The trail was clear, but I stifled the urge to quit marking the signs.

I was so intent on finding blood drops that I was nearly on top of the pile of entrails before I noticed it. The sudden realization of what had happened brought a flood of rage, disillusionment, and frustration washing over me. The drag path was clear and fresh. I had no doubt that it ran to the empty section of road where the truck that I had heard leave shortly before had been parked. I ran to the road in a futile attempt to catch a glimpse of the now vanished vehicle.

Hurrying to my car, I threw my gear in the back and took off to the check station, hoping to catch him there. I played what had probably happened repeatedly in my mind as the car hurtled along the road. He never took a shot, so he must have known that the buck could not get very far when he first saw it. My guess is that he heard my gunfire close by and rose from his seat. He probably saw the does running too far out for a shot, and sat back down.

Then, seeing the buck headed toward him over the crest of the hill, he rose again. He likely was aiming when the buck went down; collapsing a final time a few yards from him. I can also picture his frantic rush to field dress and drag the buck out of the woods before I arrived; all the while casting furtive glances in the direction from which he knew I would come.

A hunter yelled a profanity at me as I sped by him. It broke the spell of my temper. I began to picture how stupid I would look if I roared up to the check station many minutes after my antagonist, leaped from my car, and accused, I knew not who, of stealing my deer. I stopped the car and sat for a while regaining my composure. Then, I backed down the road to the hunter I had just past. When he saw me coming, he took several steps off the road and brought his gun up across his chest in a defensive gesture. More precious minutes passed as he returned my apology with an angry lecture on how to drive. Only then did he give me the chance to explain my plight. In response, he told me that he had heard, but not seen the truck as he was coming out of the woods.

Resigned now to the fact that I was likely too late, but still intent on trying to catch my unknown assailant, I drove on to the check station. No one was there but the game warden. He listened sympathetically, but could not offer me a description of the truck or the hunter that I was after. He said that several hunters had arrived almost together, checked deer and left. The game warden was none too thrilled with my intention to confront my unknown assailant; so I suffered a lecture and warning from him. I had not really expected to catch the guy, but I still felt very defeated.

This was a singular event in my life as a hunter. I felt both the exhilaration of a unique hunting experience and the bitter disappointment of having my prize stolen. It devastated my unrealistic vision of what hunting is truly about. For several seasons thereafter, I worried about what would happen to my quarry when it ran out of my sight. Quick and intense on the trail, I pushed hard to find the deer. In the process, I sacrificed precious chances to enjoy my surroundings.

Fortunately for me, I had grown up in the woods. The beauty and mystery that had beckoned me as a boy still whispered their call on every breeze. Gradually, I came to realize that the man who stole that deer had not taken nearly as much from me as he had from himself. He was there to take a deer by the fastest means possible, then to return to his world and display it as an emblem of his prowess. His prize was cheap, and his memories likely marred by guilt and the fear of being caught.

It is ironic, but this hard lesson, learned through adversity, has proven to be one of the most rewarding of my life. I grew to understand that the only lasting pleasure gained from hunting comes from the hunt itself. Now, every hunt is a good hunt and every season is a success. A longer wait before I fill my tag means that I have more time to appreciate the wondrous sights that are set before me. This is when expectation rouses primal instincts that heighten the senses and make me most keenly aware of my surroundings and myself. I live more in those minutes than in hours spent in the world I left. My heart beats faster, my ears detect the slightest noises, my eyes catch the smallest movements even at the periphery; previously unnoticed odors tang in my nostrils, and the very air becomes heavy on my tongue with the heady flavors of the woods.

The kill ends the chase and anticipation. It brings on the work of field dressing and dragging the animal out of the woods. The responsibility to get the carcass checked in and processed takes me out of the woods and away from camp and the camaraderie of my hunting partners.

Before you undertake your next hunt, ask yourself "Why am I going?" If your complete answer is "To kill deer," you should probably stay home. You most likely will not enjoy your day. You will most certainly not create cherished memories.

16

THE UNANTICIPATED

I hunted deer on federal ground in Georgia for a few years. One opening day of gun season, I walked in along a logging road at about 5:30 in the morning with my hunting buddy and a stranger. About 100 yards from the authorized vehicle parking area, the stranger loaded his scoped rifle and entered the woods on a game trail to our right. We continued toward our chosen hunt area. After only about five or six minutes, we heard the stranger fire five fast shots. It was so dark that we were using flashlights to keep from stumbling in the rutted road. Startled, we stopped and look at each other with "What the heck was that?" expressions, then shrugged our shoulders at his evident stupidity for shooting at spooked deer in the dark; and proceeded to our stands. Nothing else happened and no further sound was heard.

When the sun finally rose, we were shocked to see that the woods we planned to hunt had been commercially harvested during the week between our last scout and this, our first hunt that season. There was nothing but barren, churned dirt for over 100 yards to a huge berm of smoldering tree stumps, limbs and branches; which stretched across our front for at least 300 yards. I was hunting with a shotgun, so I knew that I would get no shot that day. But my buddy was sitting in a climbing stand almost 20 feet above me with his scoped 30-06 rifle, so we hunted until lunch. He saw one buck around ten o'clock that walked into and across the field to the far side of the tree berm. The buck was distant. My buddy never got a shot before it disappeared behind the berm. We waited in hope for two hours but he never reappeared. Later, we talked about how strange it was for him to apparently bed down so close to smoking timber.

The temperature was way up by noon and a breeze had really picked up; so we packed it in and returned to our truck. That was when we saw a huge feral sow hanging from a tripod hoist. The stranger with whom we had walked in was sitting on his tailgate eating lunch. He said that he was walking along the trail while carrying his rifle pointed down and forward; and holding his small flashlight against the forestock (fore end) with his hand. As he maneuvered a slight turn in the trail, he saw some piglets in the light and heard the sow grunt. He raised his barrel, and with it his light, just in time to see her charging him from about 20 yards away. He kept the light (and barrel) on her head and shoulders as best he could and emptied his rifle. She collapsed less than ten feet in front of him. He then said that it took him almost a half hour to calm down; and what seemed like the rest of the morning to field dress and drag the sow to his truck.

He told my hunting partner that he had seen hogs when hunting the area before; so he carried the Remington Model 742 Woodsmaster, rather than a bolt action 30-06 like my buddy. My buddy traded his bolt action in on a Woodsmaster shortly after that meeting. Neither my hunting partner nor I had an inkling that wild hogs were in those woods. Needless to say, we never hunted there again without loading our weapons almost as we exited our truck.

Feral hogs have been reported in at least 35 states. Their population is estimated at over 6 million and is rapidly expanding. Keep that in mind when you plan to enter the woods.

I got into the habit of entering the woods after full daylight while deer hunting in North Carolina. There were two incidents that drove that decision. The first was seeing a rather large, mounted, black bear boar at the Game Warden's Office (and check in station) at Marine Corps Base Camp Lejeune; and hearing of how it came to be placed there. It was a conversation piece and proof source to all who hunted on base that they needed to stay awake on stand.

During that time, when Camp Lejeune hosted deer hunts the hunters were organized into parties numbering about twelve; and taken very early by truck to hunting stands erected around the hunt area. The stands were platforms that stood eight feet high and were painted international orange. They sat in and overlooked brush and overgrown fields bordering swamp land. Each hunter was required to remain on the assigned stand for the entire duration of the hunt. No one was allowed to leave the stand for any reason - no excuses were accepted. The reason for these rules was that when all of the hunters were on stands, hound dogs were released to chase the deer out of the swamp. The hunters had to shoot the deer as they ran through thick cover nearby. Because of the style of deer hunting that was employed, oo size buckshot was the only authorized ammunition.

If a hunter shot at a deer, Marines who were assigned to work for the Base Game Warden were sent to find that deer's carcass. When the deer was recovered, the hunter tagged it and got to claim the meat. If a hunter did not want the meat or could not keep it for lack of storage, the venison was donated to the local food bank. If a Marine shot at a deer and missed, then that Marine's shirt tail was cut off - starting at the shoulder blades! No, I never lost a shirt tail.

The story about the mounted bear went that a young Marine who had never hunted before was talked into going deer hunting with a group of his barracks buddies. Apparently he fell asleep soon after he arrived; while sitting on the stand with his legs dangling over the side. Just before sunrise, he was awakened by a severe pain in one of his feet. When he looked at that foot, he saw that a bear had his boot in its mouth. In a panic, the young Marine emptied all five rounds of oo buckshot into the bear's head and shoulders at point blank range. The bear collapsed and died at the foot of the stand, slumped against the ladder. The Marine was said to be still shaking around lunch time, when the hunters were gathered from their stands. He is also said to have adamantly refused to leave the stand until the bear was removed; and never hunted again.

My own experiences with black bears while I was deer hunting were not nearly as exciting. But I do find hunting to be unsettling in bear territory. I hunted an area off base by invitation of my then hunting buddy - a fellow Marine who happened to be a native of the region. We had scouted the hunt area and noticed bear claw marks about seven feet up on the trunks a number of trees; so we knew that a boar was in the vicinity. I had never hunted anywhere that contained bears. My only "experience" with them was through nature shows.

I had never seen wildlife show aggression toward humans, so I was not concerned until the first time I went to my deer stand in the dark. I could very clearly hear the bear huff-grunting and snapping its teeth together as he smashed at brush just out of my vision. Disconcerted, I decided to try an afternoon hunt next. That boar "saw me out" of his territory, just at dark, with more of his same antics.

After those experiences, I only entered those woods after I had "shooting light." Even then, he showed his displeasure by huff-grunting and swatting brush in thick cover just beyond my view at odd times through the day.

Another reason that I prefer to enter the woods only after I have enough daylight to see clearly is the nearly ubiquitous trip hazards. Fallen limbs and logs can appear on a trail literally overnight. Further, I have stumbled in ground hog holes, rabbit warren holes, and fox den holes while walking the woods in the dark.

Wildlife that is suffering from rabies or distemper will attack you when they would normally flee. Again, better to see them in the daylight than to try to avoid them by stumbling around in the dark. Admittedly, these are rare hazards, but I prefer to avoid the chance of a leg or ankle injury - or being bitten. In the same vein, inspect the deer that you harvest for blue tongue and other diseases. There is no sense in getting sick because of inattentiveness.

Remember, when you venture into the woods, you are entering the home turf of a host of wildlife. I have hunted in Michigan, Illinois, Indiana, Kentucky, Tennessee, North Carolina, South Carolina, Georgia, and California and seen venomous snakes in all of them.

I have been annoyed by angry birds swooping around trying to drive me away from a nest I did not notice. I have also been chased off a ground stand by swarming fire ants. Hornets, yellow jackets, wasps and wood bees are also insect hazards of which to stay mindful.

I have a friend who was seriously injured when he fell out of his stand while being attacked by a raccoon. He had unknowingly set his stand just under a raccoon den in a tree. Maybe momma was very aggressively defending her kits; maybe the coon had distemper - who knows...

I once had a squirrel rampage over me from my head to my boot while trying to escape a hawk. As I had no idea that either animal was around until that shocking moment, that incident startled the daylights out of me. As an aside, I have had squirrels and chipmunks walk across my boot and small birds land on my hat and shoulders, while I sat at the base of a tree waiting for deer.

I cannot count the number of times that I have sat in impotent frustration and listened to a squirrel incessantly scream or a bird endlessly screech alarm calls. The locals do NOT like intruders!

Weather is always a variable that will affect your hunts.

Most of the time it will manifest as changing pressure fronts that you do not notice but will affect the movement habits of the wildlife around you. Occasionally, you will get drenched from an unforeseen rain squall; but more often your hunt will be ruined by wind - the hunter's bane.

Even if the deer do not smell you, shifting wind will cause them to move in different directions and higher winds will cause them to lie in cover - in which case you will never see them. An unpredicted temperature drop may catch you needing warmer clothing. A sudden snow-storm can leave you stranded and in need of shelter.

Anti-hunters are yet another aggravation - and one that seems to be growing in seriousness each year. I have seen people walking through the woods yelling, beating on drums, blowing whistles and slapping sticks together. I have found my ladder stand torn partially down. I have found excrement at the base of my stand. I have never had anyone other than a Warden confront me, but I know other hunters who have had that experience.

Most states have laws against hunter harassment; but anti-hunters are passionate people who know that there is little chance they will get caught and prosecuted.

I hunted at a state park where the Park Ranger annually conducted an orienteering course in the woods during opening weekend of deer season - and prohibited hunters from using the park even if no one signed up for his event. I have had the same game warden repeatedly walk to the base of my stand and check me for proper license (*and safety equipment*); while talking loudly.

Hunting is a sport wherein the participant faces many unique challenges. If and when you hunt, be observant, measured in your actions and persistent. Above all, please be patient. In spite of the unanticipated circumstances that you will inevitably face, it is an exceptionally rewarding sport that benefits you, wildlife of all types and the community in which you live.

17

WHAT HAVE I LEARNED?

There is nothing quite as inspiring as watching the sun rise through snow covered pines on a clear, frosty, winter's Sunday morning. God provides cathedral landscapes that man can never begin to match for beauty and serenity. The music is provided by the birds. The quiet at prayer time is without comparison. The solitude feeds my soul.

Nothing soothes the psyche like sitting in a fall woodlot listening to birds and watching wildlife go about their daily lives - while knowing in the back of your mind that a deer can step out at any moment and send your adrenaline levels soaring. The combination of relaxation and anticipation juxtaposed as they can only be on a deer stand is unmatched anywhere else in life.

Lasting friendships born of shared memories of sometimes exhilarating and often times frustrating experiences are the closest form of camaraderie I have found outside of military service overseas. There is something about the fun of sharing camp that feeds a deep seated id need. The physical work of clearing a campsite, chopping wood, building a log fire (and swapping lies around it), dragging and dressing deer each satisfy an instinctive need for a sense of accomplishment that is nearly impossible to find in our high tech, fast paced lives.

I get positive feedback more quickly in that setting than anywhere else. Then the feeling of belonging, derived from the acts of the sharing of the camp chores, and the discomforts and challenges delivered by the elements and nature, the venison (and, maybe, squirrel) and the memories just are unachievable in any other venue.

Two of my deer hunting buddies and I had a tradition of cooking the last of the previous year's venison for supper the night before opening day of each gun season. By that act, we put ourselves on notice that we needed to succeed; or we would not eat venison for a year. This brought hunting back to a level of seriousness more respectful of the game we pursued. Both have passed on; but I have the memories of our times together to help fill the void of their losses. I remember them each year as I have that meal of the last of last year's venison.

I have read countless articles addressing how to determine where large bucks, particularly the alpha bucks, will be during the various phases of the rut timeframe. I have gained a huge amount of pleasure and some information from these articles. But my personal experiences have informed me that if I simply locate the does the bucks will come to me. Where did that buck go when he suddenly disappeared from its core area? He went looking for love - or something like it, of course. Find the does and the bucks will be nearby fighting each other and trying to impress the girls.

I avoid bedding areas like the plague! In my experience, mature bucks are exceptionally shy creatures. If I venture close to the places these bucks prefer, I, invariably, drive them out of my small hunting area. I practice what one might call "scout and scoot" forays. At season end each year, I thoroughly explore those places that I suspect hold or have recently held mature bucks.

When I find fresh signs of activity by mature deer, i.e.; scrapes, rubs, tracks, beds (in that order) I mentally mark those areas "toxic;" and give the deer their privacy.

I set trail cameras along the routes that I believe lead to and from their core spots; and let the lens inform me about activity through the year.

You may be handsome, but your face shines like a new dime in the woods. Wear your choice of face covering. By the way, "Dior Sauvage Eau de Toilette" is *the* current attractant for the two legged ladies - but if you wear it within two days of deer hunting the four legged ladies will avoid you like you have the plague. AND, do not use "Irish Spring" or the like when bathing to hunt. A host of manufacturers offer scent suppressants in a variety of forms. I still like unscented soap and baking soda... try them when you are out of the other stuff.

With the exception of the occasional, stupid, spike buck, deer, generally, do not move around when it is windy; they lay about in thick cover. You will, most likely, have a long day of scenery views if you hunt on a stand on windy days.

Deer like to lie between the rows of corn on windy

days. These are good times to still hunt standing corn fields. Still hunting is basically a style of hunting that its name implies. You walk, but you spend about 10 times longer being still and observing (and smelling the air) than walking. It is suspense filled hunting.

WITH WRITTEN PERMISSION OF THE LAND OWNER...

Ideally you will be able to hunt a field where the wind is blowing parallel to the rows of corn. Enter the corn field perpendicular to the rows at the down-wind end of the field. Raise your weapon to a "ready" position; step, *slowly*, into the first row looking in each direction as you enter. Stop, wait a few minutes, then bend at the waist, slowly stick your head between the corn stalks and look both directions into the next row. Be alert and observant. Sniff the air. If you smell something that resembles a dirty, wet dog or a goat (if you are familiar with their odor) a deer is close by. Step slowly into the row you just searched. Repeat that process until you have crossed the field.

Once you have crossed the field, walk about 25 to 30 slow, cautious steps along the corn rows, into the wind, pivot, and enter the corn again. You can hunt corn fields in a cross wind also, but be careful to walk only about 10 to 15 steps before you reenter the corn rows. Repeat the field crossing process until you have crossed the field again. Move into the wind as before, enter and repeat until you have covered the entire field. If or when you see deer, inch into the row containing the deer, take careful aim, and fire.

The noise in the corn will cover your noises, the wind in your face will cover your scent and the movement of the corn leaves will cover your movements - if you go *SLOWLY*.

You have a fifty-fifty chance the deer will be facing away from you so they may not have any idea you are near.

Whenever you hunt, I strongly recommend that you dress in multiple layers of light weight; loose fitting clothing that you can remove easily. Be certain to wear quality foot gear that provides adequate ankle support and insulation - ideally something that wicks moisture to allow your feet to stay reasonably dry.

People hunted successfully for millennia before camouflage clothing was offered for sale. Sitting very still is vastly more important than tree patterned clothes. A flighty fashion plate will never see the deer that are watching him or her from 50 to 100 yards away.

Most of my successful hunts have occurred while I sat on a bucket at the base of a tree; ideally one of at least two or three trees standing closely together. Pick a tree within *your* accurate shooting distance from a deer trail, which offers a clear view for at least a short portion of that trail, and sit. Have a Zen experience with that tree - become one with it and move only your eyes. Bambi and / or his sisters will wonder by within range. When that happens, move like a tortoise and get your gun sights on their vitals.

Orange is a great color. Blue is a major no-no! Basic black is perfect for inside a ground blind.

Hunting disciplines a person. Let me explain; using myself as an example. I am in my seventies; I have a host of medical issues that come with being a 70 something year old American male. It would be all too easy for me to use those aches and ailments as reasons/excuses to sit down, slouch back and not try to maintain a reasonable semblance of physical conditioning. But if I want to hunt, I must be able to walk a fair distance while carrying (say 20 pounds of) gear. I must maintain at least a modest level of upper body strength. I must be able to bend and stretch. I must be able to get down on my hands and knees - and rise lifting a modest (say up to 20 pounds) amount of weight in gear.

Accurate shooting requires that I keep my weapons in good working condition and constantly practice using each weapon that I anticipate using during the various deer weapon seasons (shot gun, rifle, muzzle loaded rifle, hand gun, compound bow and/or crossbow).

I must also preserve any hunting stand or blind I plan to use; and ensure that it (or they) is (are) clean and in good condition. That goes for a deer carrying cart, too; if I plan to use that. In short, I must "stay in shape;" I must walk and exercise in the off season. I must maintain my gear.

Just before I turned 40, I had back surgery. My deer dragging days were over. I built a cart. Today quality deer carts are reasonably priced. I highly recommend that you buy and use one.

Deer season a year after my open heart surgery found me kneeling on the ground field dressing two deer. I was not used to that level of effort in the amount of clothing I was wearing due to the cold; I hyperventilated. ...But my hunting partner thought I might be having a heart attack and called EMS. I had a tough time convincing them that I was okay; and did not need to be transported to the hospital. That incident caused me to realize that I did not breathe properly when bent over while kneeling on the ground. Now, I drag deer to my truck and place them on the tailgate. It provides an almost ideal locale, at a reasonable height, for me to field dress deer.

Lifting a deer carcass onto the tailgate can be a challenge, so I bought a hoist that I can mount near the tailgate and use to lift deer.

Seeing the expressions on people's faces when I take my truck with bloody tailgate to the car wash is a hoot! Yeah, I have a twisted sense of humor...

So what? So do not let challenges keep you from hunting. My oldest hunting partner was 92!

I was in my late 50s at the time and he called me "Youngster" and made it a point of honor to out walk me up and down terrain while rabbit hunting. You do not need to stop hunting simply because you have reached a certain age. Do not talk yourself into that and do not let others talk you into that - no matter how well meaning they are. Stay with the sport as long as your health will allow; and you will live a longer and more satisfying life.

I have hunted long enough that you would reasonably think I could gather all the gear I need without thought. WRONG! I use a checklist - and you should too. I never travel very far to hunt, so my checklist does not include "travel" items. Here is a list of the items that I recommend that you carry when you hunt:

1. The appropriate **license(s)** for the season.
2. The proper weapon; whether that is a Rifle, a Shotgun, a Muzzleloader, a Pistol, a Compound or recurve Bow, a Crossbow, or something with which I am not familiar. House and transport that weapon in an appropriate case. Some states require trigger or chamber locks - check! Be careful NOT to violate local and state laws regarding the

transportation of firearms and ammunition
jointly.
3. Appropriate ammunition for your weapon.
4. Documentation of permission to hunt. This
varies by state. You must comply!

*Check state hunting regulations annually for each state where
you plan to hunt; and ensure that you comply for each weapon
and ammo type you plan to use. Read the entire document carefully for all compliance requirements.*

AND:

Carry with you into the field:

- *License* and Holder
- String/Zip Ties for License
- Pen/Marker
- First Aid Kit
- Pocket First-Aid Field Guide
- Hand Warmers
- Compass/GPS
- Hydration system backpack (full)
- Rain Gear
- Lighter/Matches
- Rope
- Flashlight/Extra Batteries
- Shooting Glasses
- Backpack
- Gun/Bow Hoist
- Scent Killer Cover Scent

- Deer Lure/Scent
- Estrus/Fawn Bleat Can
- Grunt Tube/Call
- Snort/Wheeze Call
- Rattle Bag/Antlers
- Shooting Stick/Bipod/Tripod
- Face Mask
- Balaclava
- Binoculars
- Binocular Harness
- Rangefinder
- Arm Guard
- Bow Sling
- Knife/Multi-Tool
- Hunting Knife
- Knife Sharpener
- Processing Kit/Knives
- Deer Cart/Drag Folding Saw
- Game Bags
- Gutting Gloves
- Pelvic Saw

By the Way, do NOT neglect your license(s)!

These are "the bare essentials." This is by no means a comprehensive list; nor am I representing it as such. Use it as a starting point. Add what you know you will need based on your hunting location, game type, season of the year and local hunting weather conditions. Inevitably, I have forgotten to list something important that you will encounter.

Murphy's Law states that if something can go wrong, it will go wrong; and at the worst possible time. I know from personal experience that this law is immutable! So, plan for disaster... By that I mean:

- Carry a compact kit with a Tourniquet, Compression Trauma Bandage(s) and a Rollup Splint(s) to treat severe cuts, broken bones, joint sprains and even gunshot wounds.
- Carry two emergency sleeping bags and an emergency bivy tent
- Carry fire making materials; including two flares to start wet wood fires
- Carry enough food for an "overnight" stay
- Carry a loud whistle

NOTE: When hunting, your cell phone becomes emergency equipment. Carry it where it is secure, unlikely to get broken and easily accessible when you are lying on the ground.

Common sense is an essential hunting and survival skill. Use your common sense and good judgment; and be prudent in the field:

- Do not hunt without having an appropriate license to hunt in your possession. Many hunters get in trouble with game wardens every year because they either did not buy a license or hunted without a license they had bought. This is the fastest way I know of to lose your weapon, your vehicle, a large amount of money from your bank account, your ability to hunt in the future and your liberty, because you could spend time in the local jail. You will gain a criminal record; but that is very seldom helpful.

- Do not smoke in a tree stand and throw lit butts on the ground or you will find yourself sitting above a forest fire.
- Do not use alcohol or drugs while hunting. Guns and booze or drugs will get you or someone else killed.
- Do not take alcohol (just a couple beers or a flask of "body warmer") with you in your tree stand or you will likely find yourself hospitalized with broken limbs, a concussion, a broken back or all of these. Worse, a search party could find your corpse.
- Do not fire every shell in your automatic or pump shotgun as fast as you can. You may hit a deer with the first shot, but you will be firing into the trees with the other shots. Spraying shotgun slugs and praying that you will hit a deer means that you are as likely to kill your hunting partner or someone you did not know was there as the deer. If you just cannot control that urge, buy and use a single shot shotgun.
- One accurate shot from a shotgun, or any other weapon authorized for deer hunting, is more than enough to kill a deer. Using a single shot gun forces you to do the things necessary to make that one shot count.
- Do not fire your weapon unless and until you

are aiming at a spot on the deer's chest just behind the front leg nearest to you. A better way to aim is to aim at the front leg opposite of the side of the deer that is facing you.

- If you are elevated, aim to hit a spot low on the deer's opposite chest area abutting the far front leg. If the deer is quartering away, you may actually shoot behind the rib cage on the side of the deer near you to get the projectile to penetrate the deer's vitals.

- Do not range a deer from a stand without accounting for the height of your stand. When shooting from a tree stand, the deer will always appear to be farther from you than it actually is for shooting purposes. Without going into the math, you can resolve this problem by measuring and marking various distances from your stand tree to other trees - while on the ground during the scout and selection process. Mark trees with trail markers that you can easily see from the stand tree to indicate various ranges.

- It is never a good idea to shoot at a deer with a bow or crossbow when the deer is more than 30 yards away in the woods. Modern crossbows, and some modern compound bows, shoot their projectiles at very high speeds; however, limbs, twigs and weeds between you and the deer - that you do not notice or do not believe are in the projectile's flight path - will cause you to miss your shot; or, worse, wound a deer in a non-vital area.

- The rounds from smaller caliber, high powered rifles, including everything up to 30-06 caliber will be deflected if they strike small limbs and twigs - even leaves - also. Pick your shooting lane carefully. Stick to 100 yards or less in the woods to make consistent kill shots.

- Shotgun slugs and big, (comparatively) slow moving rounds from 45 whatever caliber or heavier "brush gun" type rifles are not affected by the small stuff in the woods. But they are limited in range by their rounds' trajectories. Stick to 100 yards or less in the woods to make consistent kill shots.

- Hopeful shooting will scare the deer and could get someone you do not see killed.

- Deer do not like the smell of an outdoor toilet. Cover your scat and urine!

- Walking the woods looking for deer is an effective way to drive deer to other hunters; but will rarely, if ever, provide you a shot. Pick a stand and STAY.

- Wandering around in the woods during gun season can get you killed!

- Do not wear solid brown, single piece, work clothes as hunting gear. Many men wear this attire when working outdoors in the winter. Some use them as deer hunting attire. I very nearly shot someone who was wearing just such garb while inching through thick cover along a deer trail that I was watching one foggy morning. Deer have light brown to reddish brown coats in summer that turn dark brown or grey as winter arrives. This hunter, who never saw me, and I were hunting during the late bow season that follows all of the gun seasons. By this time of year, I expect deer to have their dark coats; therefore, while at full draw, I held my shot until I could clearly determine if I was about to shoot at a deer - which I was not! I still get an unsettled feeling when I remember how close I came to tragedy that morning.

- Broadside shots at deer require patience, but are the preferred shots to take. The other "makeable" shot is the quartering shot. The deer will be facing toward or away from you at some angle. The quartering away shot is the superior shot. Aim at the deer's lower chest area next to the front leg opposite you. To choose an aiming point, visualize the projectile's path to the exit point on the deer's far side. Then, aim at the spot on the deer's near side that lines up with the exit point. Gun hunters can take a quartering toward shot; but that shot offers a very small target area and usually leads to a single lung hit which means a long track and damage to a lot of meat. No hunter should shoot at a deer that is moving directly away as the chances of a clean kill are extremely small. Even a lucky shot will result in extensive meat damage.

- Bow hunters should not attempt a quartering toward shot. The deer will see or hear you when you shoot and "jump the string." By that I mean that deer can duck nearly any arrow.

They can take flight with uncanny speed at the slightest hint of danger. A deer collapses its front legs and drops its chest to the ground preparing to spring, reflexively ducking below the arrow. As soon as the deer is down, it will start to turn away from the sound that startled it; preparatory to a leap and bounding flight with tail held high.

- Based on scientific tests with penned deer, it takes an average of about one-sixth of a second from an unnatural sound, like an arrow release for a deer to start moving. The average whitetail stands between 36 and 40 inches high at the top of the shoulder.
- The typical the kill zone (the heart-lung area) is about 10 inches high. They can drop 12 to 15 inches in about one-quarter of a second.
- Even when taking a broadside shot with archery equipment, it is only possible to aim for the center of the kill zone without worrying about the deer dropping much when shooting less than 20 yards. Aim increasingly low on any shot past 20 yards.
- When you shoot a deer, expect it to run away. Stay where you are! If you are hunting from an elevated stand, be aware that the landscape will look very different at ground level. Study the trees, foliage and terrain features. Find some landmark that you will be able to recognize on the ground. Descend. Mark your location so that you can easily find it if needs be. Study the forest. Locate landmarks and or noticeable

traits about the trees around where you saw the deer when you shot. Look for knot holes, odd shaped or a broken limb, possibly the tree leans or part of a tree is dead. Find something that you can readily recognize when you are standing away from your stand tree. Walk as directly to where you saw the deer as you can while maintaining as much eye contact on where the deer was as you can.

- When you arrive; search diligently for any sign that you wounded the animal - then mark that sign in some highly visible way (a sheet of toilet paper). Wait at that location for at least one-half hour. Move slowly and search thoroughly for more sign of the injured deer; marking each sign as you go. Continue in this vein until you find the deer.

- Do not get lazy and quit tracking after a few minutes. You have a legal and moral obligation to search for wounded prey.

- If you need help tracking, mark your spot in some fashion that will allow you to find it when you return, then go get your hunting partner or someone else who is competent to help you locate the deer.

- Many hunters have been severely gored and sometimes killed by "dead" deer. Do not rush up and grab it by the antlers! If you see your deer lying on the ground, approach it very cautiously from behind. When you are near enough, poke/prod/ jab or in some similar fashion try to provoke that deer to rise and run.

If the deer does not react to your actions, check to make certain that its eyes are open... unconscious deer can awaken and hurt you badly. Dead deer always have open eyes. Shoot the deer again if it lives.

- Do not forget to tag your deer! You must display the license tag in a visible fashion; set forth by state regulations. Be careful to comply with State law concerning tagging, reporting and transporting your deer.

- Dead deer are heavy. Do not try to drag it if you know that you have a heart, respiratory or other cardio/pulmonary condition - go get help. If you do drag the deer, take your time and take frequent rest breaks. People die every year while dragging deer from the woods.

- I never had a problem field dressing deer, because I grew up gutting small animals of all types - and deer are simply a larger version of the same thing. However, if you have not had any experience, it is important that you watch some YouTube videos on the process before you go on that first hunt. Rubber gloves and a sharp knife are the only essentials for the process. Understand, though, that field dressing a deer is awkward work and the carcass will be difficult to handle and drag. Be advised, you will experience new "aromas" your first time.

Another quick check of the internet will prove the information in this and the next paragraph. Hunting is a privilege granted by the citizens of the state and nation in which you hunt. It is regulated by those citizens through their elected representatives. The legal control of wildlife, as recognized under the state ownership doctrine, is based on the fundamental premise that state government has the power to control the taking (by capturing or killing) of all wild animals found within their jurisdiction. This power is exercised under the broad concepts of police power, but is mixed with public trust concepts.

Note that the doctrine is not based upon the claim that the government owns the wildlife as an individual might own a dog or goat; rather the state is regulating the actions of citizens.

All forms of hunting are serious endeavors. There are no acceptable excuses for ignoring or acting flippant about your duty to conduct yourself responsibly. Your bad behavior could easily cost everyone the loss of the hunting privilege cherished by your fellow huntsmen.

NEVER minimize:

- Your personal safety
- The life of other hunters - both seen and unseen by you in the field
- The life of the animal you are trying to harvest
- The life of any other animal that you will also encounter
- The concerns that your loved ones harbor for you
- The property of others
- The habitat into and through which you journey

I found a listing titled: "The Four Rs of Ethical

Hunters." at www.coursehero.com. I invite your attention to that site and article. The four Rs therein listed are:

- Respect for Self
- Respect for Others
- Responsibility for Actions
- Respect for Resource

18

TROPHY HUNTING

We deer hunters are taking lot of heat about our sport. Trophy hunting is a prime example. Deep in our hearts, we are all trophy hunters to some degree. It is time that we gave some thought to what we are doing.

I see trophy hunters as falling into four categories. First is the hunter who owns a large, maybe even trophy size, mount that took years of pursuit to acquire. Memories of many trips to the woods come flooding back each time that the hunter looks at that animal. The hunter relives all those times that the animal "out smarted" him. Maybe on opening day, after the hunter had been out watching him since the previous January, had seen the buck in the spring, wearing velvet, had seen the antlers grow during the summer, and was awed by the beautiful rack that had emerged in the fall. He knew the buck's favorite trails from his bedding area to the feeding plots. He had spent days or weeks slipping around in thick brush in the buck's core area, who knew everything that a human can about a specific deer, only to be defeated by a sudden change in the buck's habits when the hunting season opened. Now, after years of trying and failing, the hunter has the deer in his home to be admired and remembered for the magnificent animal that he was; and all of the cherished times that the hunter shared with him.

We all know trophy hunter two. He is us; or our hunting buddy, who got lucky one season. We retell his story every year, secretly hoping that his good fortune will happen for (or again for) us. He is the hunter who has a "lucky" rack; the person who was in the right place at the right time; by accident - and knows it. The one who unexpectedly found a large, maybe even trophy size buck, right there in plain view and unaware of danger; and harvested it with an accurate shot.

He is the hunter who can still clearly remember the flood of adrenaline that hit his system causing trouble even focusing, much less aiming his weapon. The guy who was so nervous that his whole body was shaking. The one who almost forgot to raise the gun or who could barely aim because his eyes kept drifting back to view the entire animal. He may have gotten a fat lip or a bruised shoulder when the weapon went off because he could not concentrate enough on holding the weapon properly. Who, after firing, was amazed to see the buck collapse. The one who ran to the buck, yelping with joy and astonishment. Every time that he looks at that buck, this hunter remembers all of these things. He has a sense of deep appreciation for those incredibly special seconds during which he was more alive and aware than at any other time in his life. This person's bond with the animal, now represented by that rack on the wall, will last a lifetime; unexplainable, but more powerful than any bond of kinship that he ever developed with any pet.

Third is the elite, amateur trophy hunter. He was in the woods and felt much of the excitement that the first two felt, but no strong bond developed between himself and his quarry because he had invested little of himself in the hunt. He knew that if he missed, the guide whom he had paid to place him on this deer's trail would do it again for this or another deer the next day.

He is more a shopper than a hunter. Often the deer that he has chosen to shoot has been selected from several of admirable size. The trophy rack is the end result of a commercial venture that has been managed to provide entertainment and a degree of challenge with a tangible prize as the reward. It feeds the ego, but not the soul. The hunter has shallow memories, mere shadows of those carried by the first two types of hunters, which usually emphasize his prowess more than respect for his prey.

The fourth hunter is the cynic. He has gone hunting strictly for the entertainment value. Occasionally, he will not even go into the field. When he does, he frequently trespasses and damages property. His hunt is for excitement and revelry. He pays for pleasant surroundings, good food and drink, the challenge of cards and other diversions; and a rack to take home and tell a tale about. The deer has little value to him, and the rack, likely purchased pre-mounted, is a souvenir. His partner is the poacher who killed the deer at night or out of season and mounted that trophy strictly for sale. We hear rumors, and occasionally read stories, about hunter four. We are ashamed of and for him and ourselves, because he portrays himself to be one of us. He leaves a bad taste in our mouths, but we never do much about him or his partner the poacher.

Infrequently, hunter number one will make his passion his profession, and we will read his articles or watch his videos. He teaches us the skills and mechanics needed to be more successful during deer season, but he rarely shares his deep feelings about deer. We also see him with hunter three on television. He is the guy who we all know made the hunt a success, but he doesn't talk about all of the time that he searched, or when he failed, or just sat and watched with great admiration.

We don't hear much about the tremendous amount of effort and money that he and the rest of us have invested in developing habitat or saving wild areas from commercial development. We aren't told about the enormous importance that hunting license sales has in supporting State and Federal wildlife programs. Instead, we read stories or watch broadcasts about poachers and abusers, or wildlife officers who are protecting the animals and the public from us! We are paying their salaries, yet more often than not they treat us as probable offenders when we meet in the field!

An old cliché states, "The best defense is a good offense." If we are to have any chance at winning the battle for our very existence in which we are engaged, we must stop standing apart, grousing among ourselves about the steady erosion of our rights, and become wholly engaged in a multifaceted campaign.

Let's face it; those who want to get rid of us have some arguments that merit attention. We must get rid of the poacher and the abuser, and pressure trophy hunter four to either get serious about the sport or find another way to amuse himself. We must also convince trophy hunters one and three that they must use the power of the media to present a more complete picture of what it means to be a hunter to the public at large.

We must meet with wildlife enforcement officers on neutral ground and establish a close working relationship. Further, we must support organized efforts to reach out to our communities with an honest, positive message concerning our sport; and our contributions to the recreational and wildlife areas that they enjoy so much. These things must be accomplished while avoiding recriminations against our detractors and confrontations that serve only to place us at a disadvantage.

If we are as committed to our sport as we claim, we will face the fact that abuses occur and we are as guilty as the perpetrators if we stand by doing nothing. We must police our ranks, stop littering, respect the property rights of landowners, and, most importantly, quit tolerating hunter four and his partner the poacher.

Further, we must break our deadly habit of dismissing our detractors, usually with an oath, and start listening to the truths and honest complaints hidden in their rhetoric. We can find common ground if we approach them with patience, honesty, the willingness to sincerely listen, and a desire to establish understanding. If we fail to take these first steps, hunters will be as hard to find in the woods as old Tom turkey much sooner than any of us is willing to imagine.

Hunting is an honorable endeavor that has been pursued by every culture on earth for thousands of years. Once, a scant hundred or so years ago, many members of our society depended on hunters for their very survival.

Today, we are a nation of city dwellers. The size of the urban setting varies dramatically, but 90 percent or more of US citizens live in or very near a metropolitan area of some population. Farmers and ranchers are about the only non-urbanites in this country anymore.

With the growth of commercial slaughter of domesticated animals to provide meat for masses of people, hunting has fallen into disuse by the public in general. We hunters no longer seem necessary. Never an enterprise for the faint hearted; hunting is now looked upon by the majority of people as unnecessary; and a minority of people as abhorrently violent, if not outright criminal.

City dwellers have always been both fearful and distrustful of those who venture into the unknown to do violent acts, even on their behalf. We are perceived as the proverbial wolves in sheep's clothing that must be forced out of the flock. I believe that we are the guard dogs; but dogs and wolves look basically alike to sheep. Now we are either a threat, because we know how to use instruments of violence and demonstrate a willingness to do so; or a source of envy for some perceived power that others want to strip from us.

We, like the wolf, bear, and puma, are an endangered species in this country. Unless we unite, do far more to police our own, speak with a strong voice about the many beneficial things that our money and efforts provide, and remind our representatives that we too have rights; we will beat these animals to extinction.

AFTER ACTION REPORTS

How is it that I can remember deer hunts with such clarity and detail? I wrote each of these stories shortly after each hunt; as a literary form of After Action Report (AAR). Wikipedia defines an AAR as any form of retrospective analysis on a given sequence of goal-oriented actions previously undertaken, generally by the author themselves. Literary AARs can be formal or informal documents.

I define stupidity in two ways: as either doing the same thing repeatedly and expecting a different outcome; or knowing that you should not do something, but doing it anyway. If you don't conduct these reviews after each event - if you don't try to learn from your mistakes, you will never improve. I review the hunting stories I have written before each deer season; and I have always been willing to share them with anyone who is interested in learning from other people's mistakes. Interestingly, I have previously gotten very few "takers" of my offer.

According to Wikipedia (again), the first AARs were

developed by army generals. One of the first and best examples of an AAR is Julius Caesar's "Commentaries on the Gallic War;" and states that contemporary examples of AARs include project evaluations in business, as well as summaries of large gaming sessions in videogame culture.

Obviously, these stories are not structured in any way like a military document, but they can be used to achieve the same goal - improvement of hunting skills. The two principal forms of AARs are the literary and analytical. The analytical seeks to improve performance while literary seeks to improve style. In most cases, AARs are a combination of both types when used in a vocational setting.

Most analytical AARs are conducted over a contemporary problem or situation that has occurred in the past is happening right now, or what could happen in the future. While I served with the Marines, I was habituated in my early adult life (ages 20 to 40) to writing plans of action for events. We called them Five Paragraph Orders. Then, when each event was completed, I wrote an AAR to analyze the management of the event by identifying strengths to be maintained and built upon, as well as identifying potential areas of improvement. Lastly, I would gather the leaders involved in the event and we would participate in an After Action Review. This meeting provided an opportunity to assess what happened and why; by addressing the questions:

- What was expected to occur?
- What really occurred?
- What went wrong and why?
- What went well and why?

The goal was to apply the lessons learned. The number one thing is performance; and it should be your only measuring stick. If someone's performance was substandard, it may not necessarily have been this person's fault. Recognize in poor performance the need for more or better quality, training; and make it happen.

On a Totally Different Topic

I offer a few, short articles for your consideration...

20

YOU ARE SO VERY SPECIAL!

You are unique in all history. No one has ever lived - or ever will live - who is exactly like you. You are worthy: worthy of love from God; worthy of forgiveness by God; and worthy of an intimate relationship with God. You are worthy not because of whom *you* are or what *you* have done; rather because of whom *Jesus*, the Christ, the Messiah, is and what *He* did for *you* ... And so is everyone else!

> John 3:14-18 "Just as Moses lifted up the snake in the wilderness, so the Son of Man must be lifted up that everyone who believes may have eternal life in him." For God so loved the world that he gave his one and only Son, that whoever believes in him shall not perish but have eternal life. For God did not send his Son into the world to condemn the world, but to save the world through him. Whoever believes in him is not condemned, but whoever does not believe stands

condemned already because they have not believed in
the name of God's one and only Son."

God loved you so much that He gave His only Son, who
was born fully human as Jesus of Nazareth, Israel. This
Jesus willingly died a terrible death in payment of your
sins. He did not die to save you; that would have taken
your authority to choose the path of your eternal life. He
accomplished something far better. Jesus took on your sins
and gave His life in your place so that you could have the
ability to freely choose to love Him, have faith in Him and
follow in His ways; thereby achieving the right to spend
eternal life with Him and God, the Father of us all.

You are not the only cause of Jesus' death - each person
who has ever lived or will ever live is equally responsible,
we each put Him on that cross with our sins. But it was
NOT a collective act that Jesus performed for us. He sacrificed for each and every one of us *individually*!

Jesus loves you so much that if you were the only
person in all history to have ever committed a sin, He
would have gladly still taken your place on that terrible
wooden cross and paid your sin debt to God, the righteous
Father of all humankind, to give you the ability to choose
eternal life with Him - or without Him.

So, you see, you are VERY special. Jesus willingly laid
down His human life in your place; but the grave did NOT
keep Him. He rose! He lives! And He wants to have a
loving, personal, intimate relationship with you! He is
there, beside you all of the time. You need only believe in
Him, confess your sins to Him and ask His forgiveness. ...
And know that if you are sincere, He WILL FORGIVE
YOU.

The Bible teaches that we consist of body, soul and spirit: *"May your whole spirit, soul and body be preserved blameless at the coming of our Lord Jesus" (I Thessalonians 5:23)*. Our material bodies are evident, but our souls and spirits are less distinguishable. Your soul is yours but your spirit belongs to God. The Greek word for soul is psuche. This word implies our mind, will and desires as seen in our personal preferences, choices, and emotional responses to life's situations. Our soul is reflected in our personality. The Greek word for spirit is pneuma. It refers to the part of man that connects and communicates with God.

Our spirit differs from our soul because our spirit is always pointed toward and exists exclusively for God, whereas our soul can be self-centered. The joy, comfort and peace of God's presence can only be experienced through our spirit. While everyone's soul is fully active, not everyone's spirit is, because when Adam sinned, the spirit died within him and he was separated from God. Only in Christ is the spirit reconnected and reconciled with God, the Father: *"At one time you were separated from God. But now Christ has made you God's friends again ... by his death ... "* *(Colossians 1:21-22)*

You are an immortal soul in a temporal body. Someday, your temporal body will die and slowly turn to dust. And at some future date that only God knows, your soul will be called to stand before Jesus; and be held to account for choices it made while occupying your human body. If you were "born again" of the spirit while your mortal body was alive - if you knew Jesus and loved Him during your mortal life - you will spend eternity with His in your next, immortal and eternal, life. If you refuse Him in your corporeal life, your soul will be forever separated from Him in your unending life in Hell.

The choice is yours. If you have not already made the decision to walk with and love Jesus, you only have this lifetime to make that choice. And remember, just like you never know when you fall asleep in this world, you do not know when your soul will fall asleep; and your temporal body will die. You DO NOT own the future. Do not wait - choose!

Deep down, do you believe that you are special in a way other I have discussed? What makes you so special? Is it your holiness and ability to see when others have gone astray? "He who is without sin, let him cast the first stone." Remember, forgiveness of sin is an act of grace through faith in Jesus, so that none can boast. Is it your exceptional degree of sin for which not even Jesus can or will atone? "Today, you shall be with me in paradise." "Father, forgive them for they know not what they do."

Maybe you are like most people, no one special, not a judge of others, not a huge sinner, just not yet ready to lay everything at God's feet. Regardless of whether or not you think that you are special, you are. In the movie "The Music Man," the kids played their instruments poorly. The sounds that they produced could hardly be called music. To most listeners, it was cacophony - but not to their parents, who sat, focused and adoring, and listened raptly to their child. As if that child was the only instrumentalist in the room. God is the same way. He absolutely loves to hear the sound of your voice. What really makes you so very special is that God loves you, so much that He gave Jesus the punishment you rightfully should receive. "For God so loved the world that He gave His only begotten

Son, that whosoever believes in Him will not perish, but have everlasting life." The punishment is done. Jesus took your punishment to give you the freedom to go to God. God and Jesus have done what they needed to do to save you.

Now it's your turn. God eagerly waits for you to come and say, "I was wrong. I'm sorry. Please forgive me."

Be thankful for what Jesus did for you, take Him as your Lord and Master, tell God sincerely and with a contrite heart what He so wants to hear, restore your relationship with Him or you will face your own just punishment on judgment day and eternal separation from God thereafter.

Remember, you only have your lifetime in which to act and no one else can do this for you. Who can absolutely guarantee me that he will awaken in the morning? Or that he will sleep tonight? Procrastinating can cost you eternally. Will you be born twice to die once or born once to die twice? It's your choice. Decide!

Please, do not choose to isolate yourself from love forever - knowing that you made the wrong choice. Choose eternal bliss with Jesus and God our Father. God has your optimal life plan available for you to choose; and He gave you free will. You control your future. Choosing to live your life by God's plan will give you the best possible future.

In the remainder of this life, remember to always say only what you mean. Don't be afraid to express yourself honestly and forthrightly. If you love someone, tell him or her. Stay close to your friends and family, for they have helped make you the person that you are today. Reach out NOW and tell someone what he or she means to you.

Resolve all conflicts with others now; to the maximum extent that you are able. Because when you finally decide that it is the right time to do so, it might be too late. Seize the day. Never force yourself to say, "I wish I had." Those are among the most tragic words that you can ever utter.

Ephesians 2:8, 9 "For it is by grace you have been saved, through faith- and this is not from yourselves, it is a gift from God – not by work, so that no one can boast."

21

FROM EDEN TO NOD

*This is "Just John," but I submit it for your consideration...
take it for what you think it is worth.*

On the sixth day, God created Adam from the dust of the earth and breathed life into his nostrils. He placed Adam in the garden and commanded him not to eat from the tree of the knowledge of good and evil. God then decided to provide a helpmate for Adam. He took a rib from Adam's side and created Eve. God then made them man and wife. He blessed them and commanded them to be fruitful and multiply, filling the earth. God gave them, and all animals, every seed bearing plant for food.

God rested the next day - giving us the seven day week; not measurable by any temporal means.

Mid-morning on the Sabbath finds Eve standing in front of the one tree in the entire garden that was forbidden her. Well, maybe it was and maybe it wasn't, after all, wasn't it only her husband who had told her what God had said? How credible a source was he?

Eve had a conversation with a serpent. That seems strange indeed to me, but she apparently found it quite normal...so did Adam. Then, "After she had eaten some of the fruit, she turned and gave some to her husband, who was with her, AND HE ATE IT." The fool was standing beside her the whole time and he did nothing to stop either the serpent or his wife! In fact, Adam must have lead Eve to the tree. God had not told her where the tree was situated.

Why would Adam do what God had told him the afternoon before not to do? Eve was God's perfect creation – no woman has ever been more beautiful. Adam had just spent the night with her obeying God's command to "be fruitful and multiply." This was the first morning of their honeymoon. If any man in history was in the "Anything you want, dear." mood, it was Adam.

Adam had a perfect brain. He was the most intelligent man who ever lived. Eve's perfect brain made her the most intelligent woman who ever lived. They graphically demonstrate that intelligence does not necessarily beget sound judgment.

Because of their disobedience, Adam and Eve were cursed, along with all of creation, and cast out of the garden. Death took sway over the entire universe. The creatures created on days five and six could now kill each other to eat. Plants could develop poisons and thorns... some could even become carnivorous.

The next fact that we are told is that "Adam lay with his wife, Eve, and she became pregnant and gave birth to Cain." Since both were perfectly healthy, and God wanted them to fill the earth, it is very reasonable to assume that Eve became pregnant very shortly after leaving the garden - if not while still in it! Adam and Eve were likely less than one year old when Cain was born... and less than two years old at Abel's birth. They had many other sons and daughters in subsequent years.

When Adam was 130, Eve bore him a son whom she named Seth, saying, "God has granted me another child in place of Abel." Given the state of Adam and Eve's health, there is absolutely no reason to believe that they were barren for 128 years. A far more likely scenario is that Eve was mourning the recent loss of Abel when Seth was born.

If Abel was murdered when Adam was nearly 130, then several other facts can be logically deduced. Cain and Abel would each have been over 125 years old when the homicide occurred. They were virtually perfect physical beings with equally healthy sisters to take as wives. Therefore, they almost certainly were the fathers of large clans encompassing at least five generations when the murder was committed.

Estimating a modest average family size of six, Cain and Abel could easily have been the patriarchs of families numbering over 9,000 each. A patriarch takes his family when he travels. This would explain why Cain needed to build a city when he moved to "the land of Nod." Nod is the Hebrew root of the verb "to wander". Therefore, to dwell in the land of Nod can mean to live a wandering life. Instinctively knowing that the thousands of descendents of Abel would want revenge would have given Cain ample reason to fear for his life and have his family build a walled citadel.

Some have suggested that Cain took his wife from

among "other people" living in Nod who were not descendents of Adam. This would negate the message of salvation. Once again, the serpent is sowing the seeds of doubt in hopes of harvesting more souls with poor judgment. There is no need or other reason to propose this mythical people. The plain truth is that Cain took his wife, most likely his sister, possibly a niece, and family with him from Eden; siring Enoch shortly after arriving. God did not prohibit the marriage of siblings until the time of Moses.

22

AROUND THE CORNER

BY CHARLES HANSON TOWNE

I offer a poem from the public domain by Charles Hanson Towne and another by an Unknown Author (with which I have taken license) for you, whoever you may be, who have taken your time to read this far. Enjoy each, think about each; then reconcile with someone, renew that old friendship, be happy and know that you are blessed.

Around the corner I have a friend,
In this great city that has no end,
Yet the days go by and weeks rush on,
And before I know it, a year is gone.
And I never see my old friend's face,
For life is a swift and terrible race,
He knows I like him just as well,
As in the days when I rang his bell.
And he rang mine, but we were younger then,
Now we are busy, tired men.
Tired of playing a foolish game,

Tired of trying to make a name.
"Tomorrow" I say! "I will call on Jim
Just to show that I'm thinking of him."
But tomorrow comes and tomorrow goes,
The distance between us grows and grows.
Around the corner, yet miles away,
"A telegram sir," "Jim died today."
That's what we get and deserve in the end.
Around the corner, a vanished friend.

23

MOMENTS IN LIFE

AUTHOR UNKNOWN

There are moments in life when you miss someone so
much that you desperately want to pick them from your
dreams and hug them for real!

If you can, do not wait, reach out and touch them.

Reconcile if needs be... seek forgiveness if needs be; forgive
if needs be!

The happiest of people do not necessarily have the best of
everything;
they just make the most of everything that comes along
their way.
When one door of happiness closes, another opens;

but we often look so long at the closed door that we don't
see the one that has been opened.

Don't go for looks; they can deceive.
Don't go for wealth; that fades away.
Go for someone who makes you smile,

because it takes only a smile to make a dark day seem
bright.
Find the one that makes your heart smile.

Dream what you want to dream; go where you want to go;
be what you want to be,
because you have only one life and one chance to do all
the things you want to do...

But be careful that you stay on the path God has set
for you-

for that is the ONLY route to true happiness.

May you have enough happiness to make you sweet,
enough trials to make you strong,
enough sorrow to keep you human, enough hope to make
you happy

and enough faith to make you eternally blissful.

The brightest future will always be based on a forgiven
past;
you cannot go forward in life until you let go of your past
failures and heartaches.

Forgive!

When you were born, you were crying and everyone
around you was smiling.
Live your life so at the end you are the one who is smiling

and everyone around you is crying.

ABOUT THE AUTHOR

JOHN PEYTON is a lifelong hunter and outdoor enthusiast. He grew up in central Illinois, but left when he was 20; returning thereafter only for short visits.

He served in the United States Marine Corps for the next twenty plus years of his life. While in the Corps, he hunted on or near virtually every duty station to which he was assigned.

John has hunted in California, Georgia, Illinois, Indiana, Kentucky, Michigan, North Carolina, South Carolina, and Tennessee.

He married the former Connie Watkins (a "hometown" girl) in 1971. They are blessed with a son, a wonderful daughter-in-law and five grandchildren.

He has a Master of Arts degree from Webster University and a Bachelor of Science from Southern Illinois University.

Made in the USA
Columbia, SC
18 November 2020